CILT The National Centre for Languages

Speak up!

Getting talking in the languages classroom

15

Young Pathfinder

er Satchwell with June de Silva

First published 2009 by:
CILT, the National Centre for Languages
111 Westminster Bridge Road
London SE1 7HR

www.cilt.org.uk

Copyright © CILT, the National Centre for Languages 2009.

ISBN-13: 978-1-904243-67-0

A catalogue record for this book is available from the British Library.

Printed in Great Britain by Hobbs the Printers Ltd.

CILT Publications are available from Central Books, 99 Wallis Road, London E9 5LN.
Tel: 0845 458 9910. Fax: 0845 458 9912. Web: **www.centralbooks.com**

*** I would like to dedicate this book to Eric Hawkins ***
(Emeritus Professor of Education, York University) who has been my language
teaching 'guru' for over 30 years. He has always been an inspiration and a guiding
light to so many of us in the language teaching world, constantly reminding us of aspects of
learning that we had forgotten – or probably never even though about before.
It is with pleasure that we have been able to quote some of his wise words
on several pages of this book.

If in the next few years we can develop in our primary schools a really thorough education
of the ear and an enjoyable apprenticeship in learning how to learn languages,
I am sure no-one will be more delighted than he.

Peter Satchwell, February 2009

Acknowledgements

I owe a real debt to June de Silva without whose help and encouragement this book would never have been rewritten.

My thanks are also due to other friends and colleagues:

- to David Hicks for sharing with me his thoughts on the value of music and rhythm in the primary languages classroom;
- to our various editors at CILT, but especially to Alex Bridgland for helping to make order out of chaos in the first draft manuscript;
- to our critical readers who undertook the vetting of the draft manuscript – especially to Joan Dickie whose incisive and thought-provoking comments were much appreciated.

Peter Satchwell, February 2009

CILT would like to acknowledge the assistance of the Consejería de Educación at the Spanish Embassy, London for providing the Spanish examples used in this book.

» Contents

» Introduction

Speak up: Getting talking in the languages classroom (YPF14), based on *Keep Talking: Teaching in the target language* (YPF4), an earlier title in this series, has been completely rewritten with the aim to offer encouragement and support to all those primary class teachers who are embarking on the teaching of a foreign language for the first time.

Since *Keep talking* (YPF4) was written in 1996 there has been a dramatic change in government attitudes to languages in primary school. The impetus to put languages into the primary curriculum came from the Nuffield Languages Inquiry whose final report: *Languages: the next generation* (2000) urged the government to introduce languages from age seven on a national scale.

Many of the Nuffield recommendations have now been adopted and the publication of the *National Languages Strategy* (NLS) in 2002 set primary languages on a firm footing and brought England into line with its European neighbours.

The Languages Review Consultation Report (December 2006) urged the government to make languages a statutory component of the Key Stage 2 (KS2) primary curriculum from 2010 for the first time, and now, we have a commitment to four years of planned language learning in KS2 curriculum time for every child in primary school.

We have endeavoured to meet the needs of all those non-specialists who will form the majority of primary languages teachers in the next few years. We hope that we have also provided more ideas and food for thought for those primary teachers who have been teaching a language for some time.

Although language learning is not a compulsory part of the Key Stage 1 (KS1) curriculum we have included some ideas and suggestions for this age group as so many schools are already successfully introducing a language before the age of seven.

Just as oracy precedes literacy in children's learning of their mother tongue we should not expect children to produce the new language with any confidence until they have had a lengthy immersion – a *bain linguistique* – in which to acclimatise their ears (and, subsequently, train their tongues) to the sounds and rhythms of the new language.

We would expect therefore that in most primary classes:
- At KS1 teachers will concentrate on Listening, Speaking and Social Interaction (Oracy) with a gentle introduction to the printed word e.g. reading and recognition of captions, simple rhymes and song texts.
- At KS2 teachers will gradually and systematically introduce reading of familiar words, sentences and, in Year 5 and Year 6, short texts.
- Writing will be used initially as a support to memorising texts that the children already know orally and then built up throughout KS2.

This book makes frequent reference to:
- The KS2 Framework for Languages Parts 1 and 2 (DfES, 2005), Part 3 (DfES, 2007).
- The Primary Languages Training Zone: **www.primarylanguages.org.uk**
- The revised QCA Guidelines and Schemes of Work for Languages at KS2 (Qualifications and Curriculum Agency, 2007) in French, German, Spanish: **www.qca.org.uk/qca_11752.aspx**

The KS2 Framework for Languages sets out clear learning objectives from Years 3 to 6. It is not language specific but it shows how to ensure that your pupils' progress over the four years and it provides a host of ideas for classroom activities.

We would strongly urge all primary schools in England to use the KS2 Framework for Languages and the Primary Languages Training Zone to inform and support their language teaching at KS2. Teachers will need ample time to absorb the methodological and resource implications of the four-year programme, as set out in the Framework and demonstrated in the many examples of good practice on the website.

Primary schools will of course need to liaise closely with other primaries in their area and with their nearby secondaries over choice of foreign language(s).

Teachers who are introducing a language at KS1 would do well to consult Section 6 of Part 3 of the Framework (p85 ff) in order to prepare their children for further language learning in KS2.

The Primary Languages website **www.primarylanguages.org.uk** is designed specifically to provide primary teachers with free guidance, practical ideas for the classroom and dozens of clips of sample lessons and lesson plans from all over the country, showing what can be done in KS2. Video clips are included in six languages: French, German, Spanish, Italian, Mandarin and Japanese.

Teachers will find invaluable help on methodology, use of the new language and classroom activities in the Support and Guidance Zone, the Teachers' Zone and in My

Zone, where you can save resources from the site. The Leaders' Zone on this website which will also prove useful when working with colleagues in school.

Further work on the teaching of community languages is currently being undertaken with a view to publishing similar guidelines to those in the KS2 Framework.

» Why teach young learners in the new language?

Outlined below are some of the arguments for teaching as much of the lesson as possible in the new language, but how much of the lesson is conducted in the new language and how much in English will depend very much on the age of the children and the skills and confidence of the teacher. The Primary Languages website illustrates in the video clips a range of approaches to using the new language in the classroom and you will need to decide which style of teaching best matches your own capabilities.

» Teaching in the new language

Advantages

- Ensures immersion in the new language for the maximum possible time, giving pupils the opportunity to assimilate the language subconsciously.
- Enhances the pupils' listening skills – makes them listen attentively.
- Enhances pupils' powers of concentration.
- Introduces new sound combinations and intonation patterns.
- Encourages mimicry.
- Encourages new body language and mime to express meaning.
- Gives opportunities for total physical response in mime, gesture and actions to convey understanding of new phrases without the use of English.
- Provides opportunities to carry out daily classroom routines in a new language giving credibility and validity to the foreign language as a genuine means of communication.
- Provides opportunities for fun and games at a simple level, reinforcing basic skills and concepts already learnt in the mother tongue.
- Gives access to a new culture through learning new rhymes, tongue-twisters, songs, poems, raps and stories.
- Provides opportunities to participate in customs and festivals from another culture – birthdays, Christmas, Easter, national festivals.

Tips

- Give beginners plenty of time to absorb the new language before expecting them to give more than one word answers; they will produce phrases when they are ready and confident.
- Devise a system of regular praise and rewards for responses to listening as well as speaking tasks.
- Watch out for children whose attention strays unless regularly brought back into the fold!
- Keep a close eye on less able pupils who may soon get lost. Make sure all are following by using mime/visual aids to support your meaning.
- Keep constant checklists of the new language phrases you plan to use and be consistent from week to week, ensuring that you constantly recycle the structures and build on vocabulary from previous lessons.
- Reinforce the key words and phrases used orally with classroom display as an *aide-mémoire* for the children, using visuals and symbols.
- Build into each lesson regular 'check-back slots' to make sure all have understood so far. Carefully choose pupils to demonstrate an activity to the rest of the class.
- Be sure to build into your lessons a regular 'English-slot' to clear up misunderstandings, queries and worries.
- Try to avoid changing constantly from the new language into English and back – this just confuses everyone! Stick to the new language in blocks of time. Some teachers signal when they are changing over from one language to the other.

Teaching in the new language has implications for both teacher and children:

- **The teacher** needs to be competent and confident enough in the language to plan and structure his/her lessons so that there is both clear linguistic progression and constant revision for the pupils on a week to week basis.
- **The children** need to be provided with constant opportunities to immerse themselves in the new language and enjoy it, to practise and regularly recycle the language they have just learnt and ultimately to use the new language for their own purposes and in new contexts. Your pupils will only keep talking in the new language if you do!

That is not to say that every language lesson can be taught entirely in French, German or Spanish; that would be unrealistic for most teachers in primary school. There are many occasions when judicious use of English is essential, for example, to explain the rules of a game, to discuss a major cultural difference, clarify misunderstandings or simply to provide reassurance to individual pupils.

The amount of new language you use will often vary according to the content of the lesson. For example:
- If you are playing a language game using the interactive whiteboard, you should try to use as much new language as possible to bring children to the board, praise them and involve the whole class.
- Talking about celebrating birthdays in different countries would be mostly in English, but new language could be introduced if the children then watch a video of a French/German/Spanish birthday party and sing the birthday song.

If we can set up in the classroom activities which involve the children in:
- real communication – because they **need** to say something in the new language and **want** to take part;
- tasks which help to improve their general language skills – listening attentively, thinking about meanings, comparing their own language with this new one, following instructions, using simple dictionaries;
- activities that introduce them to the culture and daily life of their peers in the countries where the new language is spoken;
- we will be providing learning opportunities that will be memorable and useful for the rest of their lives.

Realistic objectives for primary school children include:
- communicating in the new language – oracy and literacy;
- development of language skills and knowledge about language – in their first language and the foreign language;
- development of language learning skills – learning how to learn a new language – language learning strategies;
- development of cultural awareness – intercultural understanding.

The KS2 Framework for Languages and the QCA Schemes of Work provide a fund of ideas that will help you to produce motivating and rewarding activities for your class. By getting children involved in games, songs and physical activities you can ensure that they and you will make regular use of the new language and gradually come to accept it as a challenging and enjoyable means of communication.

Chapter 1
» Beginning the languages' learning apprenticeship

'Learning a language is like opening the door on another world!'
(Year 5 child – quoted in the KS2 Framework for Languages)

'The unique value of apprenticeship in the foreign language is that it takes learners on a voyage of discovery, comparing the known with the unknown in terms of both language and culture.'
(Eric Hawkins – *Listening to Lorca* 1999)

In this chapter we have tried to distill the most common elements that underpin the best primary practice across Europe and the UK; and we deal with some of the factors you will need to consider when planning your scheme of work.

With young beginners, whether at KS1 or at KS2, you will need to consider how you are going to present a new language, a new code of communication in a supportive and exciting way, so that your learners are motivated to experiment with words and venture to use the new language for their own purposes. First and foremost you will need to bear in mind that:
- your pupils are embarking on the acquisition of an important life skill and you need to foster a positive attitude to language learning later in life;
- your pupils are beginning a language learning apprenticeship, one that (in England) will last at least four years – maybe six or seven if they start in KS1 – before they focus on a more intensive study of a language or languages at secondary school;
- the apprenticeship your pupils are embarking on should include not only the learning of the chosen language(s), but also learning **how** to learn a language.

Your children need to be taught:
- how to listen attentively, and how to hear nuances of pronunciation and intonation;

- how to mimic new sounds and make their tongues work accurately;
- how to interpret body language and gestures and how to commit to memory rhymes, songs, dialogues and all the key phrases that they will want to use to communicate with others, both inside and beyond the classroom.

These are transferable skills that the children will need to acquire for most curriculum areas throughout their schooling – and for life.

Their awareness of language in general needs to be enhanced by comparing the foreign language with English/their mother tongue – and with other languages they encounter in their local community. Learning how language works should also relate directly to their learning of English in literacy lessons. All languages have a structure and certain patterns which children should be encouraged to look out for. If you have bi- and trilingual pupils in your class, you can make use of this linguistic diversity by encouraging individuals to share their knowledge of other languages with the rest of the class. This will not only boost their self-confidence, but also raise awareness of how fascinating languages can be.

You might ask them:
- How do you greet each other in your language? (Politeness to adults/family? Body language?)
- How do you ask a question? (Tone of voice.)
- Teach us to count up to five/ten in your language.
- Teach us the words for colours in your language.

This is dealt with more fully in *A world of languages* (YPF10) where the authors have a great deal more to suggest on this subject.

The object of our apprenticeship is to give children a sense of enjoyment and real achievement. As Hawkins points out, they need to feel confident that they can 'do things with words', that they can communicate their own feelings and ideas and say what they want to say to native speakers and their peers abroad. So they need to be challenged to memorise and perform in the new language as often as possible – playing games, singing songs, reciting rhymes, tongue-twisters, role-playing, listening to and acting out simple stories. We want them to go on to secondary school knowing what they know in a foreign language and what they can achieve with it; being able to communicate in a limited, clearly defined number of situations.

The KS2 Framework for Languages states:

> 'The expectation is that most children will be able to reach a
> level of competence in a language(s) ... and that after four
> years of language learning most Year 6 pupils will be able
> to understand simple spoken and written language, to speak

aloud and take part in short conversations, and to write simple sentences. They will also understand about different cultures and have an idea of how languages work and how to learn them. In short, they will be becoming confident users and learners of a new language.'

The European Language Portfolio illustrates this well in the simple goals it sets out for primary children, as in the illustration below:

As we emphasise in Chapter 2, in the initial stages of language learning, oracy must precede literacy, just as it does in mother-tongue learning. Children will need an extensive period of listening to new sounds, trying to work out meanings from your use of mime and facial expressions, flashcards and visuals. Only **after** they have atuned their ears will they slowly acquire the confidence to mimic the new words and respond verbally to your questions.

» The four Cs of primary language teaching

Keith Sharpe, who for many years was closely involved with the development of the Kent Primary Languages Project, sets out some very sound advice on primary languages methodology in his book *Modern Foreign Languages in the Primary School* (2001). In his analysis of the needs of the primary languages teacher, he talks of 'the four Cs' of primary language teaching: Communication, Culture, Confidence, Context. His ideas are summarised in the table below:

Communication

Listening and Speaking for real in contexts of relevance to the children. For the teacher this means: no translating, only closely controlled reading, and concentration on Listening and Speaking.

Culture

Children must learn about the manners and customs of the foreign country as an integral part of learning the language, thereby countering stereotypes/insularity, breaking down the monoglot view of foreigners, raising multilingual/multicultural awareness and respecting the children's right to bilingualism/multilingualism.

Confidence

Pupils should enjoy their lessons and be encouraged to 'have a go'. They should not be criticised for every mistake – they must be allowed to learn by making mistakes. Pupil/teacher relationships are crucial to a positive learning environment: the teacher must be an encourager with a sensitive, tolerant attitude to error.

Teachers need confidence in using the new language themselves – but they do not need native speaker fluency! They need to provide children with opportunities for creativity: drama, making and doing in the new language.

Context

Teachers should teach as far as possible in the new language. They need a variety of realia and authentic material, and need to train the pupils' ears and tongues to new sounds and codes. **Pupils** need regular, intensive practice in the new language with songs, rhymes, games, role play and performance. They need to be able to make the new language their own – and use it for their own purposes.

Sharpe points out that, in practice, 'Primary French is more Primary than French' – good primary language teaching will give children confidence about language in general.

Sharpe's ideas correlate very closely with the key elements of primary language teaching as set out in the *Nürnberger Empfehlungen* – a set of recommendations published in

1996 by an international consortium of experts in the teaching of German in primary schools:

- The content of ELL should relate to the interests of the children and extend them.
- It should appeal to their feelings, develop motivation and imagination, creativity and enjoyment.
- Pronunciation, rhythm and intonation, non-verbal communication and body language all have an important role to play.
- Children need to realise that all languages conform to patterns and rules.
- Teachers need to create a classroom atmosphere in which children feel at ease.
- Teachers need to appeal to the whole child through a multi-sensory approach.
- Children must be constantly active and doing in the new language; so games, songs and activities including story-telling, mime and drama should form the bulk of our teaching.
- Children should get used to working individually, in pairs and in small groups.

These ideas and approaches to primary language learning are reflected in all the currently available materials from UK and European publishers. For example, in *Hélico* (2001), *Ja Klar!* (2003) and *Grandi Amici* (2001) (published by ELI, Italy; distributed by European School Books) the authors attach great importance to a multi-sensory approach which involves the learners in using both halves of the brain. As every primary teacher knows, not all pupils can learn the same material in the same way at the same speed. Children have disparate cultural backgrounds and disparate learning styles. So we should try to build into our teaching a variety of strategies and activities that play to the strengths and talents of individual pupils; they should be enabled to acquire the new language through using all their senses.

The information below is derived from the work of Howard Gardner (Harvard University Press, 1983) and illustrates how his theory of 'multiple intelligences' can be linked with classroom activities. You will find examples of many of these in the classroom clips on the Primary Languages website.

Linguistic
- Playing with words
- Relating spoken words to the printed form
- Completing gapped sentences/missing letters, crosswords, word-searches

Logical/Mathematical
- Playing with numbers
- Counting forwards and backwards
- Doing mental arithmetic
- Calculating/estimating sizes, distances, times
- Sequencing and classifying

Musical
- Singing
- Melody and rhythm
- Playing musical instruments
- Dancing – music and movement

Spatial
- Art and colour
- Visual aids
- Craft and design
- ICT
- PE, playground games and sport

Environmental
- Experiencing the natural and the built environment
- Observation, recording and drawing for real
- Seeing, feeling, hearing, smelling the world around us
- Hands-on experiences

Kinaesthetic
- Use the whole body/total physical response
- Physical activity: PE, games, sport, music and movement

Interpersonal
- Cooperative learning
- Pairwork/groupwork
- Acting and mime
- Board games, card games, circle and playground games

Intrapersonal
- Expressing personal feelings
- Sharing memories
- Making choices/expressing opinions

» Embarking on primary languages for the first time

If you are about to embark on the teaching of a foreign language for the first time, it is perhaps worth reflecting on what the children already have on board and on what they bring with them from their experience of learning their mother tongue. We know that some children may be barely literate in their own language when we introduce them to a new one, but they still have skills and instincts that we need to exploit, as Susan Halliwell reminds us in *Teaching English in the Primary School* (1992):

> 'Young children do not come to the language classroom empty-handed. They bring with them an already well-established set of instincts, skills and characteristics which help them to learn another language.'

> Children:
> are already very good at *interpreting* meaning *without necessarily understanding the individual words;*
> *already have great skill in* using limited language creatively;
> *frequently learn* indirectly *rather than directly;*
> *take great pleasure in finding and creating* fun *in what they do;*
> *have ready* imagination;
> *above all, take great delight in* talking!

> *In the early stages of their mother tongue development children excel at making a little language go a long way: intonation, gesture, facial expressions, actions and circumstances all help to tell them what the unknown words and phrases probably mean. In order to make the most of the creative language skill the children bring with them, we therefore have to provide them with occasions when:*
> *• the urge to communicate makes them find some way of expressing themselves;*
> *• the language demanded by the activity is unpredictable and isn't just asking them to repeat set phrases, but encouraging them to construct the language actively for themselves.*

> *That is why games are so important ... especially guessing games. Guessing is a very powerful way of learning phrases and structures, but it is indirect learning because the mind is engaged with the task and is not focusing on the language....'*

Here then we have the key elements of successful primary languages pedagogy. By making capital out of the children's innate urge to communicate we can encourage them to take risks with the new language, making up their own phrases – and accepting that making mistakes is a natural part of language learning.

» Preparation for teaching in the new language

As with any new class, you will need to do some thorough preparation for teaching in the new language. You will need to design a scheme of work – or adapt an existing one – mapping out the topics you intend to cover each term, and the language items (vocabulary, phrases, structures, cultural aspects) that you and the children are going to use and explore. We deal with this in Chapters 3 and 4. It is also dealt with in *A flying start!* (YPF11) p11f.

There are increasingly good classroom materials emanating from UK and continental publishers, including, for example, *Early Start French/German/Spanish*, *Rigolo*, *Tout le monde*, *Sonica*, and *Ja Klar!* Many of the well-written (and beautifully printed) primary resources from continental publishers are well worth exploring, if only to acquire a reference copy as a source of ideas. The European Schoolbooks catalogue: *Languages for Young Europeans* (**www.younglinguists.com**) offers a wide range of materials in French, German, Spanish and Italian. Most of these cover the same skill areas as the KS2 Framework for Languages.

There is now a growing source of local support for primary language teachers through Local Authorities and the CILT Regional Support Groups who offer training and advice under the 'Professional Development' tab on the Primary Languages website. You will also find an expanding supply of ICT materials from UK publishers that offer motivating consolidation activities for individuals or pairs of pupils to work through at their own pace.

The Resources library at CILT houses an enormous range of materials and details can be found at **www.cilt.org.uk**.

Chapter 2
» Listen carefully!

» Education of the ear

In this chapter we argue for providing young beginners, whether they start at KS1 or at KS2, with a period of intensive **listening practice** before expecting them to start talking. We explore what kind of listening activities are appropriate for beginners and suggest some strategies for atuning their ears to new sounds, new intonation patterns and new ways of expressing themselves. At the end of the book you will find a resource list with suggestions for further inspiration from books, DVDs, classroom resources and websites.

What do we mean by 'education of the ear?'

Eric Hawkins has always emphasised the need for children to be 'awakened' to language and find out how it works, what you can do with it and what you can achieve with it. Primary pupils need to acquire the tools for language learning and learn to do things with words, experimenting for themselves in a new medium of communication.

The authors of the KS2 Framework for Languages emphasise that:

> 'Learners need to assimilate new sound patterns and relate them
> to words and meanings. This process is particularly important
> in the early stages of acquiring a language when learning
> habits are being established – and with young learners who
> are particularly receptive to new sounds. In the learning of
> their first language/mother tongue children build up a wide
> experience of spoken language and interaction from birth and
> draw on this as they become literate. With a new language,
> exposure to the sound patterns needs to be built into the
> learning experience because listening to and manipulating

*the new language are critical to language learning. For this
to happen, learners need frequent opportunities for intensive
exposure to the new language.'*

Some authors have pointed out that children go through a 'silent period' when starting to learn a language. Sarah Phillips, for example, writes in *Young Learners* (Oxford University Press, 1992):

*'It is almost always true that young learners understand far
more than they can say, and when children learn their first
language, they respond to language long before they can speak.
Second language learners also have a 'silent period' in which
they listen to the language around them, internalise it and
formulate their own personal grammar, which they adapt and
expand as they are exposed to more [of the new] language.
Some authors argue that this period should be respected and
that students learning a new language should not be made to
speak [or write!] until they are ready, that is, until they do so
spontaneously.'*

When introducing a new language in primary school we should design in this extended 'silent period' as part of our pedagogy. Depending on the background and maturity of your pupils, this period of intensive listening may extend to several weeks before they are ready and confident to attempt their first words or phrases in the new language.

On the one hand, some children arrive at primary school with well-tuned ears and amazing ability to pick up the new sounds accurately, and in our experience it is often the children from bilingual homes who find no difficulty in getting their ears and tongues round a third language, because they are already linguistically aware and alert. On the other hand, some children from monoglot homes – where there is little or no parental awareness of the need to set aside time for one-to-one dialogue – arrive in reception classes with severe language deprivation and minimal communication skills.

For all of these diverse pupils we need to develop strategies and activities that will build up their sensitivity and alertness to the sounds and nuances of a new language – and ultimately build up their confidence to launch into this new way of communicating.

According to Eric Hawkins:

> *'Education of the ear should start at KS1 – and there is no better*
> *introduction to careful discriminating listening than learning to*
> *sing – in English and other languages, preferably folksongs ...*
> *At the KS1 stage of 'awakening' to language ... a sympathetic*
> *and imaginative music teacher is a crucially important ally.'*
>
> (Language Learning Journal 32, 2005)

We could not agree more ... as will become apparent later in this book.

At the end of this chapter we have provided a résumé of the sections of the KS2 Framework for Languages which deal with Oracy – i.e. listening, speaking and social interaction. This gives an overview of how children's learning should progress over the four years from Year 3 to Year 6. The same principles apply equally to KS1, so you can use many of the ideas set out for Year 3 but at a simpler level.

» Listening to whom?

The first source of new language that the children will hear is usually going to be your voice – in greetings, classroom instructions and directions for games and activities.

So it is important that you develop your own personal repertoire of classroom management phrases that you are comfortable with. To begin with this needs to be only a modest repertoire of simple instructions, short phrases, words of praise and encouragement, like the 'starter list' we have suggested on pp47–49.

But it is important that your class is not brought up on a restricted diet of 'teacher-speak', however good your accent is! As soon as is feasible you should introduce your learners to the voices of native speakers, so that they get used to hearing how the new language is spoken by children of their own age and in the context of their own culture – at home, in school, or out and about in town.

At KS2 the *Early Start* DVD packs are invaluable in this respect, as they are specifically designed to present the new language in an authentic context, so that your class can see and learn something of the everyday life of their peers in France, Germany and Spaing while learning, say, about mealtimes, talking about pets, or simply learning their numbers.

At KS1 you will find resources like *La ronde des petits* (1996), *Entre dans la ronde* (1996), *and the Hocus and Lotus stories* (2007), which, with careful teacher management, are motivating and attractive for early years' classes.

We cannot of course expect young beginners to follow native speakers talking at full tilt, but we can expose them gently and progressively to the new language by playing CDs/DVDs of easy songs, rhymes and poems, and simple dialogues spoken by children in contexts that they can relate to and understand. Gesture, vocal tone and facial expression will all help the children to gain confidence and arrive at meaning. There is no shortage of song material now available on CD/DVD, ranging from well-known traditional children's songs and folksongs to more modern, often humorous texts composed especially for children by such talented performers as Henri Dès or Detlev Jöcker – but you will still have to be selective and choose the simpler, slower songs with texts that are accessible to your class.

Another invaluable source of authentic language is becoming increasingly available through the British Council's programme of recruiting Foreign Language Assistants (FLAs) to work in primary schools. In 2006 more than 150 FLAs were employed in UK primary schools. An FLA working in two or three primaries can be worth his or her weight in gold; a young person from the foreign country can have a dramatic impact on the whole school and there is no better motivator for young children than to have weekly contact with a real, live (sympathetic!) native speaker working alongside you in the classroom; a precious 'walking dictionary' for you the teacher when you are stuck for the right phrase or word - and a constant source of interest to the children, who can try out their newly learnt language for real. You will find excellent ideas for working with foreign language assistants in primary classrooms in *Working together* (YPF12). You can find out how to apply for an assistant to work in your area by consulting the British Council website: **www.languageassistant.co.uk** or by email to: assistants@britishcouncil.org.

» Listening to what?

We have listed below a range of activities that we feel are appropriate at KS1 and KS2. Our initial listening should focus on new sounds, on 'sensibilisation', checking that the children have heard accurately and that they can discriminate between words and phonemes that might, at first hearing, sound the same. For example, children listening to French for the first time, may not be able to distinguish between the 'ou' in *sous*, *pour*, *amour* and the 'u' in *sur*, *pur*, *mur*.

The children will need a lot of practice in saying words with new sounds – both vowels and consonants – for example: in Spanish, the 'j' in *rioja*; in French, the 'rr' in *rouge*; and in German, the 'ch' in *ich*, *durch*.

» Activities for KS1 and KS2

Whenever you can, particularly at KS1, aim to start your lesson with a song or a rhyme, either live or on a CD/DVD. You could also begin with a story or by greeting the class puppet who is just waking up. This will signal the changeover from English to the new language. Teachers have assured us that if you play the same song often enough, you will be surprised how many children pick up the text and sing along, even though they do not understand every word. We have listed some of the best song collections in the Resources list on p137. And whenever you can, try to finish the lesson with a class performance of either a song, a rhyme or a tongue-twister – something memorable for them to take away. If the song has actions, so much the better, as this will help to 'fix' the words in their memory.

The activities we have illustrated below are all suitable for KS1. Many of them are derived from well-known party games, so you can always make up your own variations. The important thing is that the children get so absorbed in the fun of the game that they do not worry about making mistakes – or that they are practising the same language items over and over again!

KS2 activities can and should become progressively more demanding, gradually challenging the learners to spot a pattern in the new language or think out a rule. Then the games can become more sophisticated, according to the children's age and interests. For example, there is enormous mileage to be had out of games like 'Battleships', 'Word and Number Bingo', 'Hangman' and other games where the focus is now on spelling and matching the spoken to the written word; and the competitive element is always a good motivator.

» KS1 listening activities

To begin with, the simplest activities are those that let the children show with a physical response that they have understood. For example, a whole-class song with actions, such as: Mes petites mains font tap,tap,tap; or *Il pleut, il pleut, il pleut très fort*; or the Teddy Bear song (see p28):

> *Nounours, nounours, touche le nez....*

> *Teddybär, Teddybär, dreh dich um...*

The class might also learn a counting song/finger rhyme with actions:

Un bisou pour mon lapin	*Eins, zwei, Polizei,*
Deux bisous pour mon poussin,	*Drei, vier, Offizier,*
Trois bisous pour mon poulin,	*Fünf, sechs, alte Hex,*
Quatre bisous pour mon chien,	*Sieben, acht, gute Nacht!*
Cinq bisous pour mon dauphin,	*Neun, zehn, Auf Wiederseh'n!*
Des bisous, tout plain, tout plein.	

And of course your class will love miming the actions you show them: *Touchez le nez, la tête, le pied, le coude,* or showing that they know classroom objects: *Apporte-moi: un crayon, une gomme.*

They might listen to simple instructions and watch how to make something, such as a finger puppet, a flower, an animal or a spinner.

The responses we can expect from children can be described as a series of simple stages in the 4Rs of Recognition, Repetition, Recall and Real Use. We have illustrated how your class might progress through these stages as their confidence builds.

Stage 1: Recognition

This stage will require mostly non-verbal responses; the children simply show their understanding through actions or mime. Simple classroom commands need only an action from the pupil(s): *Regardez! Ecoutez! Assieds-toi! Sautez! Dancez! Frappez les mains!*

This can be turned into a game of 'Simon says' to reinforce the same items. Or the children can be asked to place a set of objects in the order they are heard, using Multilink or other classroom resources.

The Fruit Salad game is also a good opportunity for learners to show their understanding without having to speak a word. The children sit in a circle. Each child is given the name of an object (fruit, colour, item of clothing, etc). When the teacher/child in the middle calls out an item, all those who have that name must change places. If 'Fruit Salad' is called everyone changes. You can remove one chair each time, as in the traditional party game. Plenty of space is needed!

Other activities might be to:
  • listen for specific words in a song or poem;
  • clap syllables of a word;
  • place objects in the order they are heard, using Lego/Multilink cubes;
  • play miming games;
  • use mime, gesture, facial expressions to show understanding of what they have heard;
  • give a physical response to show understanding (Total Physical Response);
  • respond to instructions with a physical action (TPR);
  • sequence a set of pictures to show understanding of a story/rhyme they have just heard;
  • act out a story as it is read.

Stage 2: Repetition

This stage might require just a minimal verbal response:

C'est un/une XXX?	*Ist das ein/eine XXX?*	*¿Eso es un/una XXX?*
Oui, c'est un/une XXX	*Ja, das ist ein/eine XXX.*	*Si, esta es un/una XXX*
Non, c'est un/une YYY.	*Nein, das ist ein/eine YYY.*	*No, esta es un/una YYY.*

If you are using a puppet in class, the puppet may shake hands with a child and say:

Je m'appelle Didier. Et toi?

The child just gives his or her name. But later may progress to:

Je m'appelle Liam/Emily.

Other activities might be to:
  • listen to simple rhymes/stories on audio;
  • sing along with audio/video songs;
  • pick out words that are similar to the English;
  • play circle games to practice greetings;
  • answer questions from a puppet;
  • perform finger rhymes;
  • play guessing games – what's in my bag/what's on the card;
  • play the Fruit Salad game.

Stage 3: Recall

This stage might expect single words with accurate pronunciation, or slightly longer phrases:

Quel âge as-tu?	*Wie alt bist du?*	*¿Cuántos años tienes?*
(J'ai) six (ans).	*Ich bin sechs (Jahre alt).*	*Tengo seis años.*
Où habites-tu?	*Wo wohnst du?*	*¿Dónde vives?*
(A) Croydon.	*(Ich wohne) in Croydon.*	*En Croydon.*
Tu as un animal?	*Hast du ein Haustier?*	*¿Tienes alguno mascota?*
Oui, j'ai un chien.	*Ja, einen Hund.*	*Si, un perro.*
C'est de quelle couleur?	*Welche Farbe hat er?*	*¿De qué color es el perro?*
Marron.	*Er ist braun.*	*Marrón.*

Other activities might be to:
- respond to the register with a question or statement;
- say finger rhymes;
- rehearse simple tongue-twisters slowly, then speed up, e.g. *Fischers Fritz fischt frische Fische*.

Stage 4: Real use

This stage would expect whole phrases and sentences from your more confident pupils. You might play a game where each child has to ask a question and another has to answer.

Or you could play Chinese Whispers. The class is divided into two teams. The child at the front of each team is given a piece of folded paper with a familiar phrase written on it. On your command the two team leaders read what is on the paper and whisper it to the person behind them. The last child says the phrase and the teacher writes it on the board.

A slightly more sophisticated task might be to ask the children to mime/act out a well-known story as it is read, e.g. 'Little Red Riding Hood', 'Goldilocks', 'Meg and Mog'.

Other activities might be to:
- act out simple role-plays;
- use finger puppets to practise short dialogues;

• express simple opinions – likes/dislikes: *J'aime les chiens; je n'aime pas les chats*.

Some Local Authorities, such as Warrington, have developed a range of games which encourage children to play with sounds in the new language and learn to identify the vowel or consonant clusters that represent a certain sound: e.g. *vous, nous, sous; fünf, fünfzehn, Münze*.

At a later stage you could encourage your class to sort these new sounds into boxes so that they eventually become adept at hearing and identifying the phonemes. For example:

Sound discrimination games

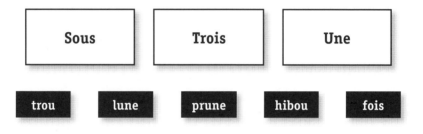

These are games that can be made up to practise phonemes that don't exist in English. For example, the children could be asked to listen for the distinction between:
• *doux/deux/du*
• *vous/voeux/vu*
• *plus/pleut/pluie*
• *fou/feu/feuille*

In each of these you might ask them to number the word of the set that sounds nearest to the word you say at the start: e.g. if you say *peux*, they should write down '2' in each case. Or you can ask them to pick the odd man out: *pain/pain/pan/pain; bain, bon, bain, bain*, initially by putting up their hands for *pan* and *bon* and later by writing the number '1', '2', '3' or '4' once they have got the hang of the game.

You may find it is simpler to ask the children to listen out for a phoneme match in a song or rhyme: e.g. *hibou/coucou; bruit/pluie*, etc.

You will find help with phonic work in classroom resources such as *Rigolo* (Nelson Thornes) and the *Early Start* CD-Rom interactive from Early Start Languages.

It is worth noting that once you have taught the children the most common colours: *rouge, jaune, bleu, vert, orange, violet, brun, gris, noir, blanc* and the numbers 1–12, you have covered most of the new phonemes the children need to hear in French – and the same applies in German and Spanish!

» Speaking activities

We have already moved on to the stage of getting the class to **repeat** what they have just heard and the children need fun activities to help them to get their tongues round the trickier sounds in the new language. By practising activities like the following, your children will be pronouncing new sounds and enjoying the activity for its own sake – i.e. indirect learning.

Greetings

You can use finger rhymes to practise greetings:

Hello (make a fist)	*Bonjour!*	*Hallo!*	*¡Hola!*
Hello, Dad (put up thumb)	*Bonjour, Papa!*	*Hallo, Vati!*	*¡Hola papa!*
Hello Mum (put up forefinger)	*Bonjour, Maman!*	*Hallo, Mutti!*	*¡Hola mamá!*
Hello brother (middle finger)	*Bonjour, frère!*	*Hallo, Bruder!*	*¡Hola hermano!*
Hello sister (ring finger)	*Bonjour soeur!*	*Hallo, Schwester!*	*¡Hola hermana!*
And me (little finger)	*Et moi!*	*Und ich!*	*¡Y yo!*
Hello (wave whole hand)	*Bonjour!*	*Hallo!*	*¡Hola!*

Counting

You could start slowly with a finger rhyme, for example:

Voici ma main, elle a cinq doigts

En voilà deux, en voilà trois.

Or a simple rhyme to the tune of 'Ten Little Indians' with animals, e.g.

> *Un petit, deux petits, trois petits lapins...*
> *quatre petits, cinq petits, six petits lapins,*
> *sept petits, huit petits, neuf petits lapins,*
> *Dix petits lapins sautent!*

The resource *Jeux de Doigts* (La Jolie Ronde) is a valuable source of ideas here.

When they are more confident the children will enjoy a song or rhyme with actions, for example:

> *Un, deux, trois, claque les doigts; Quatre, cinq, six, tappe les cuisses;*
> *Sept, huit, neuf, ouvre les yeux; Dix, onze douze, frappe les mains.*

Animals

Play or make some animal noises and ask children to mime them. There are also adaptations of the 'Old Macdonald' song in several European languages.

If you get the class to say the following after you, you are practising the nasal endings and the rise of voice on the final syllable:

> *un lapin, un chien, un poisson, un cochon.*

Or you could do a rhythmical set, to be recited like a rap:

> *Ein Krokodil, ein Loewe und ein Elefant,*
> *Ein Brummbär und ein Affe gehen Hand in Hand.*

You can practise these fast, slowly, loud or very softly – but the surest way to make them stick is to add an action to go with each animal. The children will soon invent them!

Syllables and stress

It is good practice to get the children to clap out the syllables of words.

In French they need to learn that the stress nearly always comes on the final syllable of a word – just the opposite of English.

Clapping: *éléphant, crocodile, hippopotame* ... will illustrate the point.

In German the same applies wherever they have borrowed the French word, for example: *Elefant, Krokodil, Giraffe*, but most words have the stress on the first syllable as in English: *Nashorn, Nilpferd, Eisbär*.

In Spanish there is more variation, but you might challenge your class to compare, for example, the days or the months in Spanish with the English, and to tell you whether the stress always falls on the same syllable in both languages.

Pronunciation

In each language there are always new sounds to be heard – vowels or consonant clusters – that do not exist in English, for example:
- the French 'r' as in *rouge*; 'j' as in *jaune*; 'u' as in *lune*; 'eu' as in *deux*; 'oi' as in *trois*; 'gne' as in *montagne*; 'euil' as in *écureuil*; and the nasals 'in, an, un' as in *plain, plan, brun*.
- in German the 'ch' as in *Loch*, a slightly different sound in *ich, dich, mich*; the 'zw' as in *zwei*, and the 'z' (ts) as in *Zug*; 'schw' as in *Schwester*; and the Umlaut vowels where 'a' changes to *Bär*; 'o' changes to *hören*; and the 'u' changes to *für*.(= a French u).
- the Spanish 'j' in *Juan, rojo, junio*; the 'ñ' sound as in *España, cumpleaño* and the 'll' sound as in *amarillo, paella, tortilla*.

To liven up pronunciation practice you might have great fun playing the Mirror game, where each child comes out to say a sentence into the mirror while the rest of the class watches to see what sort of faces he or she pulls while saying it, for example:
- *Loulou aime la laitue. Les lapins mangent les laitues aussi.*
- *J'aime les montagnes en Espagne.*
- *Fischers Fritz fischt frische Fische.*
- *Zwei kleine Spatzen zwitschern in den Zweigen.*
- *Juan, Julio y Jorge tienen un conejo y un periquito rojo.*

You could also make up a good pronunciation game while introducing the children to French/German/Spanish first names, for example:

Franz, Jürgen und Jochen spielen gern Fußball

Charles, Chantal et Jules jouent dans le jardin.

There are many collections of rhymes and comptines to give your pupils good pronunciation practice, such as *101 comptines à mimer et à jouer* (Bayard Jeunesse). The following nonsense rhymes appeared in *Trampoline* (Cle, distributed by European Schoolbooks) and were recorded with delightful children's voices to encourage accurate pronunciation. The following nonsense rhymes from *Trampoline* were composed to practice accurate pronunciation. They would both be a good stimulus for children's artwork – a collage or cartoon for display.

> *Charlotte et Chantal cherchent le chocolat.*
> *Julien joue avec Jules et Julie dans le jardin.*
> *Jules est charmant, mais Charles est méchant!*

> *Au printemps, p'tites feuilles.*
> *En été, grandes feuilles.*
> *En automne, plein d'feuilles.*
> *En hiver, plus d'feuilles!*

Guessing games

Children will always rise to the challenge of guessing 'What's in my bag?'. They can also be invited to feel what's in it! Once they have played the game a few times, they can then be invited to hide something in their own bag and get their partner to guess what it is. This is a good game for practising asking questions.

A variation could be to guess the picture on a flashcard you are holding; or you could do a slow reveal game, where you show only the ear of an animal, or part of an object and the class has to guess what it is. The interactive whiteboard comes into its own here (See *We have the technology!* YPF14).

Circle games and playground games

Whenever we get the opportunity we should up sticks and take our language lesson out of the classroom – to the playground or the field (or the hall if it is wet). Here you can make the most of playground games from many countries: circle games, counting games, skipping games, clapping games, dancing and party games adapted to language learning. There is a long tradition of such games in all European countries and we should make capital out of them.

Anyone who has read *The language and lore of schoolchildren* (Opie, I and Opie, P., Clarenden Press, Oxford 1959) will know what a lot of learning can go on in the playground in games handed down the generations – without interference from teachers. If you teach your class just a handful of these games the children will continue to play them on their own and make up their own variations. Clapping and skipping games are especially good, as the CILT Early Languages Learning DVD illustrates with a virtuoso performance by a group of English boys enjoying a Spanish clapping game with huge enthusiasm – and there are other examples on the Primary languages website. Some Local Authorities have exchanged traditional playground games with partner schools abroad. Cornwall, for example, has had a flourishing link with Spain where the children teach each other games in their own language.

As the CILT primary team have often pointed out, playground games:
- are enjoyable;
- require few resources;
- are applicable across the primary age range;
- help to develop social skills;
- bring in creativity – teachers and children make up their own variations;
- offer scope for exchange of ideas and links with partner schools abroad;
- take learning beyond the classroom.

Unit 2 of the QCA Schemes of Work has useful suggestions on playground games. We have described a small selection of such games below, because we believe they are valuable in educating the whole child at the same time as teaching the language. If you have taken part in a lively singing game, skipped or played hopscotch in a foreign language it is unlikely that you will ever forget the key phrases or rhymes you learnt to play them.

Most of these games could be played at a very simple level by KS1 pupils, but they can also be made more complex for older children. For example, 'Head and shoulders, knees and toes' involves not only memorising parts of the body, but expects good coordination and quick thinking as well, so the level and speed at which you perform it can be adjusted to any age group.

Our short list is just the tip of the iceberg. There are lots more games out there and unit 2 of the QCA Schemes of Work has many useful suggestions.

Let's start with the well-known Teddy-bear song. It demands a total physical response and is easy and fun for KS1 classes:

Teddybär, Teddybär, dreh dich um,	*Nounours, nounours, touche le nez.*
Teddybär, Teddybär, mach dich krumm,	*Nounours, nounours, touche les pieds.*
Teddybär, Teddybär spring hinaus!	*Nounours, nounours, saute en l'air!*
Teddybär, Teddybär, komm nach Haus!	*Nounours, nounours, tombe par terre!*

Then there are numerous **circle games** like *Le furet*. In this game, the children sit in a circle facing outwards. A gap is left to allow access to the inside of the circle. The child who is 'it' is given a soft animal (*le furet*) and he creeps round inside the circle and secretly drops it behind one child's back. When the song is finished, the child who finds 'the ferret' chases the child who dropped it round the circle trying to catch him before he reaches the gap. The player left standing is 'it' for the next game:

IL COURT, IL COURT LE FU-RET LE FURET DES BOIS, MESDAMES, IL COURT IL COURT LE FU-

RET, LE FURET DU BOIS JOLI. IL EST PASSE PAR I- CI. IL REPASSE-RA PAR LÀ.

In this German game one child chases another round the circle. The children in the circle must leave an entrance and an exit for the cat and mouse to chase in and out until the mouse is caught.

> *Katze, Katze sucht die Maus,*
> *sucht die Maus, sucht die Maus,*
> *Kleine Maus spielt gern im Haus;*
> *Hier geht's rein, da geht's raus!*
> *Leise, leise, kommt die Katze,*
> *Sieht die kleine Maus –*
> *Und – **hat** sie!*

The only prop you need for the following, well-known kindergarten game is a beanbag or a soft shoulder bag.

> *Es tanzt ein Bi-ba-Butzemann in uns'rem Haus herum,*
> *Es tanzt ein Bi-ba-Butzemann in uns'rem Haus herum,*
>
> *Er rüttelt sich, er schüttelt sich, er wirft sein Säcklein hinter sich.*
> *Es tanzt ein …*

The children form a circle and dance round hand in hand in the opposite direction to the child with the bag (*Säcklein*) who marches outside the circle. When he shakes himself they all stop and shake their arms, then shake their legs. Then the child with the bag does a shimmy shake and throws the bag over his shoulder. Whoever catches it takes a turn as the Butzemann marching round the outside of the circle.

In this next circle game one child is the leader. He goes round inside the circle and says three times:

Ne riez pas!/Keiner darf lachen!

The rest of the children answer:

Et ne souriez pas!/Und auch nicht lächeln!

Then the leader tries to make someone laugh by tickling his ear, pinching his nose or making faces. The group must be silent. Anyone who laughs or giggles is out. The last one to survive becomes the new leader.

Games with actions and repeated refrains

There are many well-known English games that can be played in a foreign language. For example, most children enjoy *Going on a Bear Hunt* (Walker Books Ltd, 1989), provided that the story is told at their level with plenty of drama. Told in Spanish, French or German this can be a winner if they all learn the sounds to go with the swishing grass, the squelching mud and the mad run to safety at the end! Like so many stories it comes off best when the children sit in a circle, join in the repeated phrases and do all the actions.

The enormous turnip, *Mr.Gumpy's Outing*, Kipling's *How the elephant got his trunk* and other *Just So stories* can all be great fun if the repeated sentences are reinforced with mime.

Are you sitting comfortably? (YPF3) has good ideas on exploiting well-known children's stories in this way.

One of the most enjoyable French games is the following traditional song. The text is sung until the questions: Loup y est tu? Que fais tu? which the children call out loud. The wolf replies that he is getting dressed, but when he suddenly shouts J'arrive!, everyone scatters, trying not to be caught.

Clapping games

These can be invented to practise numbers, days, months, anything you like, but as the children get older, the trickier the better, and all very good for hand/eye coordination.

Here is just one example from Steiermark in Austria:

Scherenschleifen Scherenschleifen

BP   BS   BP   BS

Ist die beste Kunst

BP   BS   BP   BS

Die rechte Hand, die linke Hand,

RR   BS   LL   BS

Die geb ich dir zum Unterpfand.

RR   BS   LL   BS

Da hast du sie, da nimm du sie,

RR   BS   LL   BS

Da nimm sie alle beide!

BP   BS   BP   BS

Clapping pattern shorthand:
BP = both hands to partner
BS = both hands to self
RR = right hand to partner's right
LL = left hand to partner's left

Counting out games

All languages seem to have their own versions of 'Eeny, meeny, miny, mo'. You will find examples on the internet. Here are just two:

Eine kleine Mickeymaus	*Pomme, pêche, poire, abricot,*
Zog sich mal die Hose aus.	*Y'en a une, y'en a une,*
Zog sich wieder an,	*Pomme, pêche, poire, abricot,*
Und du bist dran!	*Y'en a une de trop!*

Skipping games

You can collect many ideas for skipping games if you have a link with a primary school in France, a German-speaking country or Spain. Like the traditional English games, most rehearse numbers or nonsense rhymes. This is another instance of where the children can take away foreign language games and make them their own in the playground.

Hopping, jumping, walking

A simple playground game that teaches numbers is this French stepping game. Here the children have to make different kinds of step for each verse – ideal for KS1.

Pas à pas

Un pas, deux pas, trois pas, Je marche pas à pas.
Quatre grands pas, cinq grands pas, je marche pas à pas.
Six pas de course, sept pas de danse, je marche pas à pas.
Huit pas de charge, neuf pas de loup, Je marche pas à pas.
Encore un pas, ça fait dix pas, je marche pas à pas.
Mais pas un pas, ça fait zéro et je ne marche pas!

Hopscotch

Young beginners may enjoy playing hopscotch in French, German or Spanish. There are lots of variations on the court layout, but here are two:

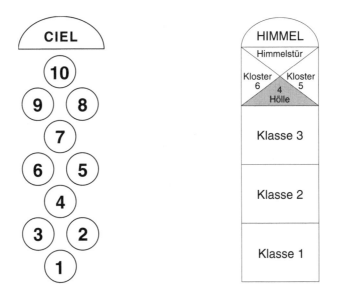

The rules are basically the same as in England, but the children must use a stone/pebble to aim at each number in turn. In the German version the players must at all cost avoid landing their stone or stepping on '*Hölle*' (Feld 4); if they do they are out of the game.

Perhaps your class might like to try out this old variation on hopscotch from Austria, *Schneckenhupfen mit Schuster* (*Le Cordonnier dans l'escargot*; *El zapatero y el caracol*). It can be played in any language; start by choosing a 'shoemaker' with a counting-out rhyme. The shoemaker then finds two stones and sits down on the ground (playground). The children draw a large chalk snail round him as in the diagram below.

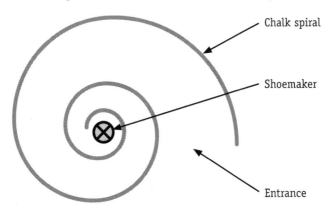

The first child stands at the entrance and shouts to the shoemaker:

Klingelingeling!

He replies:

Nur herein!/Entrez!/¡Entrar!

The customer has to hop on one leg all round the curl of the snail to the shoemaker.

If she or he steps on a line or puts the other foot down, she is out and the next player starts.

Meanwhile the shoemaker pretends to sole a shoe, tapping one stone on the other. When a customer eventually reaches the workshop, the customer says:

Grüß Gott!(Guten Tag!) Ich möcht' ein Paar neue Schuhe.
Bonjour monsieur! Je voudrais des souliers neufs.
¡Buenos dias! Quiero unos zapatos nuevos.

The shoemaker takes the customer's size by drawing round his/her foot on the ground and says:

Komm nächste Woche zur Anprobe.
Revenez la semaine prochaine pour les essayer.
Vuelva la semana que iene para probarlos.

The customer pretends to steal a pair of shoes and hops back to the snail entrance.

The shoemaker curses and chases after the customer, hopping on one foot. If he can tag the thief, the thief has to take over as the shoemaker.

» Schemes of work

You will find an enormous amount of inspiration and practical ideas for KS2 activities in the QCA Schemes of Work (French, German, Spanish) and in the recently published schemes that have been developed by individual authors and Local Authorities; we have given in our Resources List. Some Local Authorities such as Liverpool, Warrington, Wakefield, Kent and Richmond have developed their own schemes which are available free locally and on their Grid for Learning websites. You will also find free schemes of work on the Primary Languages website. Others have made their schemes available through a publisher. Whichever scheme you choose to use, you will need to study it carefully to check that it suits the needs of your school and that you and your colleagues are comfortable to work with it. You would be wise to compare notes with other schools in your area who are already using the scheme before committing school money. Most schemes come with audio CDs and soundfiles, so you will usually find audio support with classroom language and the songs and rhymes.

» The KS2 Framework for Languages: Oracy

The Framework acknowledges that Oracy – listening, speaking and social interaction – has a more prominent role in language learning than in many other areas of the curriculum. In the early stages children will spend most of their time listening, speaking and interacting orally, so they should be given regular opportunities to listen to a good model of pronunciation.

The Learning Objectives for each year begin with a summary of the expectations for learning and teaching and an overview of outcomes describing what most children should be able to do by the end of the year.

Year 3
The expectations during Year 3 are:
- Teachers will familiarise children with the sounds and speech patterns of the new language.
- Children should enjoy listening to and joining in with a range of songs, poems and stories.
- Children should learn to differentiate unfamiliar sounds and words, to mimic and play with sounds.
- Children should understand simple words and phrases and begin to repeat and to use some of them independently in simple communicative tasks and role-plays.
- Children listen to a variety of voices, which may include the class teacher, visiting native speakers, audio CDs, websites, CD-ROMs and DVDs.

By the end of Year 3 most children should be able to:
- enjoy listening to and speaking in the new language;
- listen and respond to familiar spoken words, phrases and sentences;
- communicate with others using simple words, phrases and short sentences;
- understand conventions such as taking turns to speak and valuing the contributions of others;
- learn and use correct pronunciation.

Each Learning Objective is accompanied by suggested teaching activities. These are very supportive, but they are in no way prescriptive: teachers may select from the lists or develop their own activities based on the needs and interests of their own class.

We have selected below just a few of these activities; the rest can be found in the Framework.

Year 3 Teaching Activities

03.1 Listen and respond to simple rhymes, stories and songs.
- Copy the actions modelled by the teacher or respond with a physical action when they hear a sound or word, e.g. hold up a picture card or perform 'Simon says'.
- Recognise rhyming patterns by chanting a poem or singing a song, emphasising the rhyming endings of words.
- Clap each time they hear a word which rhymes with a chosen word.

03.2 Recognise and respond to sound patterns and words.
- Respond to a particular sound with a physical action.
- Count how many times a particular sound is heard in a phrase or sentence.
- Copy a sound spoken by the teacher to practise pronunciation – for example when practising *ou* or *u*.
- Identify phonemes that are the same or different from English.

03.3 Perform simple communicative tasks using single words, phrases and short sentences.
- Respond to the register using a word or phrase – e.g. *Bonjour, madame!*
- Ask and answer simple questions using real objects, cards and games.

03.4 Listen attentively and understand instructions, everyday classroom language and praise words.
- Respond to the teacher's instructions with a physical action by pointing to something green/pink, by making a sad face, etc.
- Play 'Bingo'.
- Draw a picture or perform a mime.

Year 4

The expectations during Year 4 are:
- Children continue to enjoy listening to and joining in with a wide range of songs, poems and stories and develop their confidence, imagination and self-expression.
- They ask and answer a wider range of questions and memorise and present short texts such as finger rhymes, poems, songs, role plays or stories.

By the end of Year 4 most children should be able to:
- listen and identify words and short phrases;
- communicate by asking and answering a wider range of questions;
- memorise and present a short text.

Year 4 Teaching Activities

04.1 Memorise and present a short spoken text.
- Participate in a performance of a finger rhyme, poem or short text clearly and audibly for an audience.
- Give a short presentation, saying several sentences about, for example, the country where the language is spoken.

04.2 Listen for specific words and phrases in a song, poem or story.
- Listen to and join in with stories, songs, poems.
- Count how many times they hear a particular number, word or phrase; respond with a physical movement, by repeating the word aloud, or by piling up counters or Lego bricks/Multilink.

04.3 Listen for sounds, rhyme and rhythm.
- Listen out for plurals and give a physical response: standing up, sitting down, putting up their hand when a plural is heard.
- Compare the sound of plurals in English with those of the new language.

04.4 Ask and answer questions on several topics.
- Develop role play using puppets or props.
- Perform role play in the style of a particular character.

Year 5

The expectations during Year 5 are:
- Children listen attentively and learn to identify the main points from a short passage of several sentences.
- They enjoy listening to and joining in with a wider range of songs, poems and stories, developing their confidence, imagination and self-expression.
- They learn how to express a simple opinion and join in a short conversation.

By the end of Year 5 most children should be able to:
- pick out some detail from short spoken passages;
- enjoy interacting even when they hear unfamiliar language;
- join in a short conversation;
- make a short presentation using a model.

Year 5 Teaching Activities

05.1 Prepare and practise a simple conversation re-using familiar vocabulary and structures in new contexts.
- Use mime, gesture, facial expression and tone of voice to help convey meaning.
- Use imagination to create interesting conversations using familiar language.

05.2 Understand and express simple opinions.
- Express simple opinions using familiar vocabulary when talking, for example, about food, animals, places.
- Give a physical response to show understanding of an opinion, e.g. thumbs up for likes, thumbs down for dislikes.

05.3 Listen attentively to understand more complex phrases and sentences.
- Respond to a dictation by drawing, miming or acting out what they hear
- Repeat new phrases and sentences with clarity and accuracy, focusing on correct pronunciation and intonation.

05.4 Prepare a short presentation on a familiar topic.
- Memorise and recite a selection of short spoken texts, e.g. a song, a short poem, a set of instructions, a shopping list, a description.

Year 6

The expectations during Year 6 are:
- Children listen to texts and learn to pick out the main points and some details.
- They learn texts, sketches and dialogues by heart and perform them in front of an audience.
- They enjoy listening to and joining in with a wide range of songs, poems and stories and develop their confidence, imagination and self-expression.
- They learn to initiate and sustain conversations without help.
- They also enjoy developing short presentations or sharing simple accounts of interesting events from their own experiences using a model.

By the end of Year 6 most children should be able to:
- listen to and understand the main points and some detail from a short spoken passage;
- give a presentation in a clear audible voice;
- converse briefly without prompts;
- enjoy listening and speaking confidently.

Year 6 Teaching Activities

06.1 Understand the main points and simple opinions in a story, song or spoken passage.
- Listen attentively and re-tell the main ideas.
- Suggest an alternative ending to the story.

06.2 Perform to an audience.
- Memorise and perform a song, poem, story or sketch.
- Present ideas to an audience.

06.3 Understand longer and more complex phrases and sentences.
- Listen to a spoken phrase or sentence and act out the meaning or point to a picture card illustrating the meaning; adapt the phrase by substituting the verb, noun, adjective, adverb, etc. to change the meaning.
- Listen to and understand a range of text types from different sources, e.g. fiction, description, poetry, information, instructions.

06.4 Use spoken language confidently to initiate and sustain conversations and to tell stories.
- Sustain a conversation within the class or with visitors or via video-conferencing with peers abroad.
- Give a short prepared talk on a chosen topic, expressing simple opinions and answering questions about it.

Chapter 3
» Communication in the classroom

'Children need to talk. Without talking they cannot become good at talking. They can learn about the language, but the only way to learn to use it – is to use it!'

(Susan Halliwell, 1992)

'Tell me and I'll forget; show me and I'll remember; involve me and I'll understand!'

Old Chinese Proverb.

Our immediate aim in the primary classroom is to get the children to see that they can use this new language to say the things that they want to express by recombining the phrases and vocabulary they have learnt to create their own meanings – and that this can be enjoyable and rewarding. The aim of course is for them to be able to transfer the language and the skills they have acquired in the classroom to use them effectively with native speakers. But for the time being we have to make haste slowly, building into our lessons a wide variety of pupil activities so that the ratio of pupil talk to teacher talk is as high as possible.

If we are to create a classroom atmosphere in which children feel comfortable in the new language, we will need to take a relatively gentle approach to language acquisition. Pupils need to be encouraged to experiment with this new medium of communication, to play with words and find out what they can do with them. So we need to create a very active classroom, where children are being constantly challenged to use the new language to achieve even the simplest needs – finding where something is, using classroom equipment, asking for information, and so on. They need to be encouraged to take risks and try out the new language for themselves (as we all did in our first five years of learning our first language – for example, who cared if we got our past participles wrong 'I maked it', 'I writed it'!).

» What areas of language do teachers need?

It is widely acknowledged that you do not need to be a languages 'specialist' to teach young learners effectively (see Keith Sharpe's comments quoted in Chapter 1), and you do not need to have an encyclopaedic knowledge of the language to teach it in a primary classroom.

But it is essential that you are confident in yourself, that you can master the vocabulary and structures of the limited number of topics you have planned for the year and that you have a reasonable repertoire of classroom management language. In broad terms, you will need the language that helps you run your classroom in simple phrases and gestures that are easy for the children to understand.

In the 1990s the Scottish Office Education Department compiled a short list of 'competences' that primary language teachers should aim to acquire in order to feel confident in the classroom. The list does not differ greatly from that printed on p.16 of the Teacher's Guide to the QCA Schemes of Work in French, German and Spanish (Qualifications and Curriculum Agency, 2007).

The following are the areas of language, the knowledge and skills that teachers will need in order to manage language lessons effectively:

- The sound system (the phonics) of the language – accurate pronunciation/intonation.
- The alphabet and the numbers.
- Personal language – yourself, your family, where you live.
- Descriptive language – people, animals, clothes, town, the environment, weather, food and drink.
- Affective language – expressing likes dislikes, emotions, aches and pains, praise, terms of endearment.
- Classroom language – daily routines, greetings, instructions, praise and admonition, the language the teacher needs for organising pupil activities, the language the pupils need in order to participate.
- Language to cover activities from other curriculum areas such as maths, art and craft, PE, home economics, science, technology, drama, music, e.g. draw, colour, measure, cut, fold, stick, run, jump, catch, stand, lie, stop!
- Parts of the body: touch your left elbow/right toe, do the hokey-kokey; bring me/show me, where is/are the ...?
- The language needed to organise and play games, teach children poems, finger rhymes, songs and to narrate and act out with the children popular stories in the new language.
- Knowledge of simple grammar: e.g. gender, articles, pronouns, adjectives and agreements, possessive adjectives, present tense of common verbs, negatives, imperatives, prepositions and question forms.

» What kind of language do teachers need for classroom interaction?

On the one hand, there are all the daily routines and interactions between teacher and pupils, involving classroom organisation as well as the personal interests and enquiries of individuals. On the other, there are the specific vocabulary areas implicit in the topics you have built into your scheme of work for the year. The diagram below shows some of the kinds of language you and your pupils will need – and you will doubtless think of more.

Classroom language

Teacher

Questions to pupils	Descriptive language
What day is today? Where is our puppet hiding today.	Jackie is wearing a red jumper and a green shirt.
Answers to pupils	**Narrative**
I'll try to find out for you. I think we'll sing the song again tomorrow.	Once upon a time ...
Requests to pupils	**Affective**
P. can you open the window, please? Who can count up to 10?	That was brilliant, Jimmy! Oh what a mess!
Instructions	**Transactional**
Line up quietly, please. Will you all sit on the carpet now.	Can I borrow you ruler, please?
Explanations	**Classroom/organisational**
Person A describes the picture; Person B must try to draw it.	Time to clear up! Pack you things away now!

Pupils

Questions to teacher/another pupil	Personal language
What do we do next? When's your birthday?	What's your sister's name?
Answers to teacher	**Descriptive**
I can't find my pen.	My cat is black with white paws
Requests to teacher	**Narrative**
Can you show us how to do this, please? Can we play 'Bingo'/sing the crocodile song today?	We went to my nan's at the weekend.
Seeking help (coping language)	**Affective**
What does that word mean? How do you say (word) in Spanish?	I don't feel very well. I love dancing!
Socialising	**Transactional**
I like your new jumper. It's your turn!	Will you lend me a pencil?
	Classroom
	Where are the scissors? Can I have the glue, please?

Teacher talk

Even if you are a native speaker of Spanish/German/French it would be a mistake to use in class the same sophisticated register of language that you would use with other adults; the children would not be able to follow you. So you need to look for the simplest instructions, praise and correction phrases, the simplest explanations, the simplest question forms, using a minimum of words assisted by arms, legs, hands and facial expressions to get over your meaning – and the more visual aids you can find the better.

Here are some of the classroom situations where you are most likely to need phrases and instructions in the new language:
- Arriving at the classroom – greetings.
- Organising ourselves – seating, clothing, etc.
- Getting the children's attention.

- Taking the register, dinner money, etc.
- Starting the lesson – organising equipment/giving out materials.
- Writing up the date/changing the weatherboard/other rituals.
- Presenting a new topic.
- Setting up a pupil activity.
- Explaining again/checking that all have understood.
- Demonstrating how to play a game/playing the game.
- Ending the lesson/packing away/tidying up – saying goodbye.

These are the kind of phrases that you will need in the course of KS2 to sustain interaction between you and your pupils in the new language.

So you will need to be well prepared and confident in a limited number of classroom situations where you know you can manage the children through the new language. (And of course there will always be occasions where it is much quicker and wiser to revert to English to save time and get the job done.)

You will need to identify and learn your own 'Survival kit' of useful phrases, even if it means sticking a list to your desk as a reminder – we have all done this at some time or another! Once you have memorised your key phrases, make sure you use them consistently every week until your class knows them as well.

As your confidence grows you can slowly add two or three more phrases each week and gradually expand your repertoire.

Later in this chapter, we provide a Basic Classroom Language list for KS1/the beginning of KS2. Once you have picked from this list your favourite phrases and used them regularly in class, you may feel confident enough to slowly expand your repertoire with more variations from Appendix 1 of this book or from the many sound files now available with schemes of work and classroom course materials.

» Where to start if you have never taught a language before

Find out where you can get local training from your Local Authority, so that you are not working in isolation. When you have found colleagues from other schools to share ideas with, then you can launch into language teaching slowly and carefully, preparing your lessons with the aim of teaching a little language well and not trying to bite off more than you can chew in the time allowance you have. Fifteen to twenty minutes is soon gone, so do not worry if you have done only half the activities you planned. As long as the children can do something new at the end of the lesson, or have revisited and improved on something they learnt before, progress has been made.

What is crucial is that you have mapped out in advance the new language phrases you intend to use yourself and those you intend the children to acquire. The *QCA Teacher's Guide* (Languages: a scheme of work for KS2) suggests how you can gradually improve your performance and build your confidence in the new language by:
- scripting lesson plans: teacher language and pupil language;
- limiting teacher talk, i.e. keep it short, accurate and simple!
- using mime, gesture and visual clues to make meaning clear;
- collaborating with specialist colleagues or native speakers;
- making use of resources designed for non-specialist teachers of languages
  – the internet, DVDs, CDs – to prepare work, check pronunciation/intonation, or as a tool in class;
- improving your language skills outside school hours – listening to CDs, DVDs, spending time in the country/community where the language is spoken, attending evening classes, corresponding with a partner school abroad.

Above all, remember that your role in the classroom is to be the actor/entertainer for the children, who uses larger-than-life body language, comic gestures, exaggerated actions, in order to convey meaning and impress the new phrases on the children's memory. (If you can get your puppet (see p59), a big furry animal or your FLA to assist in this, all the better!) Practising saying words and phrases as loud as you can, in a whisper, grumpily, sadly or cheerfully, quickly or slowly, is always good fun and soon gets everyone in the class involved. As we discuss later, any physical action or visual cue that illustrates the meaning will provide hooks for the children to hang the language on.

The following list of basic classroom language is meant as a starting point for teachers at KS1 or at the beginning of KS2/Year 3. It is easily learnt by teacher and pupils, so when you and your class have mastered the phrases that you want to use regularly, you can slowly expand your repertoire by consulting Appendix 1 and the other publications from our Resources list.

It is worth highlighting at this point how important it is for the teacher to master the distinction between the singular and plural verb forms for commands. Whether you are teaching Spanish, German or French, it is tricky not to get caught out yourself when changing from addressing the whole class/group to one individual, for example:

Adam, Daniel, Jack,
asseyez-vous!
setzt euch!
Sentaos!

But:
Jessica, assieds-toi
setz dich!
sientate!

English

Greetings	Farewells
Hello!	*Goodbye!*
How are you?	*See you tomorrow.*
I'm fine thanks	*See you again.*

Introductions	Politeness
What's your name?	*Thank you.*
And you?	*Thanks very much.*
My name is X.	*Please.*
	Excuse me miss/sir!
	Sorry!

Answering the register	Getting attention
Yes, (miss/sir) Here.	*Listen!*
	Watch! Look!
	Repeat!
	Here is/this is a ....
	That is a ...... Yes or no?

Praise	Instructions
Good! Very good!	*Sssh! Quiet!*
Well done!	*Quiet everyone! Be quiet, Bernard!*
Excellent!	*Look!*
Stupendous!	*Listen!*
Cool!	*Stand up! Sit down!*
Super!	*Turn around!*
Fantastic!	*Come here!*
Fabulous!	*Go to your seat!*
Tremendous!	*Shut/Open ...*
	Quick!
	Slowly!
	Quietly now!
	Louder!
	Show me a ...
	Go on!
	Line up!

French

Greetings	Farewells
Bonjour!	*Au revoir!*
Ça va?	*A demain!*
Ça va bien, merci.	*A la prochaine!*

Introductions	Politeness
Comment tu t'appelles?	*Merci*
Et toi?	*Merci beaucoup.*
Je m'appelle X.	*S'il vous plaît/s'il te plaît.*
	Excusez-moi, madame/monsieur!
	Oh pardon!

Answering the register	Getting attention
Oui, madame/monsieur.	*Ecoutez!*
	Regardez!
	Répétez!
	Voici un/une ...
	C'est un/une ...? Oui ou non?

Praise	Instructions
Bien! Très bien!	*Chut! Silence!*
Bravo!	*Taisez-vous! (Tais-toi, Bernard!)*
Excellent!	*Regardez!*
Formidable!	*Ecoutez bien!*
Cool!	*Levez-vous! Asseyez-vous!*
Super!	*Lève-toi! Assieds-toi!*
Fantastique!	*Retourne-toi!*
Génial!	*Viens!*
Chouette!	*Va à ta place!*
Extra!	*Ferme/ouvre ...*
	Vite!
	Lentement!
	Doucement!
	Plus fort!
	Montrez-moi un/une ...!
	Allez-y!/Vas-y!
	En rang! En ligne!

German

Greetings	Farewells
Guten Morgen! Guten Tag!	*Auf Wiedersehen!*
Wie geht's?	*Bis morgen!*
Danke, gut. Sehr gut, danke!	*Bis bald!*

Introductions	Politeness
Wie heißt du?	*Danke.*
Und du?	*Danke schön.*
Ich heiße X.	*Bitte.*
Mein Name ist ...	*Entschuldigen Sie! Verzeihung!*

Answering the register	Getting attention
Hier!	*Passt jetzt auf!*
	Schaut her!
	Wiederholt!
	Hier ist ein/eine...
	Das ist ein/eine ... Ja oder nein?

Praise	Instructions
Gut! Sehr gut!	*Sssh! Ruhe bitte! Seid ruhig!*
Bravo!	*Schaut her!*
Ausgezeichnet!	*Hört gut zu!*
Toll!	*Steht auf! Setzt euch!*
Super!	*Steh auf! Setz dich!*
Fantastisch!	*Dreh dich um!*
Cool!	*Komm her!*
Fabelhaft!	*Geh auf deinen Platz!*
Prima!	*Mach ... die Tür ... auf/zu!*
	Schnell!
	Langsam!
	Leise!
	Lauter!
	Stellt euch an! In einer Reihe, bitte!

Spanish

Greetings	Farewells
¡Hola! *¿Cómo estás?* *Muy bien, gracias*	*¡Adiós!* *¡Hasta mañana!* *¡Hasta luego!*

Introductions	Politeness
¿Cómo te llamas? *¿Y tú?* *Me llamo x* *Politeness* *Gracias* *Muchas gracias* *Por favor* *Perdona (familiar)* *Lo siento*	*Gracias* *Muchase gracias* *Por favor* *¡Lo siento!* *¡Disculpas!*

Answering the register	Getting attention
Sí	*¡Escuchad!* *¡Mirad!* *¡Repetid!* *Esto es un/una...* *Es un/una.... ¿Sí , o no?*

Praise	Instructions
¡Bien! ¡Muy bien! *¡Estupendo!* *¡Fenomenal!* *¡Perfecto!*	*¡Silencio!* *¡Callaos! (Cállate, Bernardo)* *¡Mirad!* *¡Escuchad bien!* *¡Levantaos! ¡Sentaos!* *¡Levántate! ¡Siéntate!* *Vuelve* *¡Ven! ¡Ven aquí!* *Vuelve a tu asiento* *Cierra/Abre la puerta (Cerrad/Abrid el libro)* *¡Rápido!* *¡Despacio!* *¡Bajo! ¡Bajito!* *¡Más fuerte!* *Enséñame un/una..* *¡Adelante!* *¡En fila!*

» Pupils showing understanding

As we said in Chapter 2, in the first few weeks of learning a new language your pupils will be struggling to make sense of what you are saying to them and it may be some time before they begin to respond spontaneously. You need to give them plenty of opportunities to demonstrate that they have understood by giving them tasks that require non-verbal responses:
- listen and do – carry out instructions: shut the door, open the window, sit down!
- listen and do – a physical activity: touch your nose, wave your hands, turn round!
- listen and do – as the cartoon character does;
- stand up straight;
- stretch your arms;
- stand back to back, nose to nose, arm in arm, etc.

The link between visuals and classroom instructions can be developed from the outset, provided that you are consistent in using the same visual to mean the same thing throughout the learning process. Once you have taught your class a small number of instructions with mime and facial expressions, a lot of fun can be had by practising them together. For example:

	Ecoutez!	*Hört zu!*	*¡Escuchad!*
	Levez-vous!	*Steht auf!*	*¡Levantaos!*
	Asseyez-vous!	*Setzt euch!*	*¡Sentaos!*
	Retournez-vous!	*Dreht euch um!*	*Daos la vuelta*
	Reposez-vous!	*Ruht euch aus!*	*¡Echaos!*
	Dormez!	*Schlaft ein!*	*¡A dormir!*
	Réveillez-vous!	*Wacht auf!*	*¡Despertaos!*

	Regardez!	Schaut zu!	¡Mirad!
	Parlez! Racontez!	Erzählt!	¡Hablad! ¡A hablar!
	Ecrivez!	Schreibt auf!	Escribid!
	Dessinez!	Zeichnet!	¡Dibujad!
	Comptez!	Zählt!	¡Contad!
	Lisez!	Lest!	¡Leed!
	Ouvrez!	Macht auf!	¡Abrid!
	Fermez!	Macht zu!	¡Cerrad!
	Entrez!	Geht hinein!/Kommt herein!	¡Entrad!
	Sortez!	Geht hinaus!/Kommt heraus!	¡Salid!
	Avancez!	Vorwärts!	¡Acercaos!
	Reculez!	Zurück!	¡Retiraos!
	Posez!	Legt (es) hin!	¡Poned!
	Ramassez!	Sammelt ein!	¡Recoged!

Once your class has practised the actions several times you can play 'Simon says' (*Jacques a dit*; *Pumpernickel sagt*) which never fails with young children. The game can then become a regular warm-up activity at the start of lessons.

Gradually you can extend the range of instructions the children can understand, as in the visuals below:

	Ferme la fenêtre!	*Mach das Fenster zu!*	*Cierra la ventana*
	Ouvre la porte!	*Mach die Tür auf!*	*Abre la puerta*
	Ramasse les papiers!	*Sammel die Blätter ein!*	*Recoge los papeles*
	Sors!	*Geh hinaus!*	*¡Sal!*
	Danse avec moi!	*Komm tanz mit mir!*	*Baila conmigo*
	Compte de 1 à 10!	*Zähle von 1 bis 10!*	*Cuenta de 1 a 10*
	Parle à Justin!	*Sprich mit Justin!*	*Habla con Justin*
	Regarde par la fenêtre!	*Schau zum Fenster hinaus!*	*Mira fuera*
	Raconte ce que tu vois!	*Erzähl uns, was du siehst!*	*Cuenta lo que ves*
	Ecoute la cassette!	*Hör dir die Cassette an!*	*Escucha la cinta*
	Lis le journal!	*Lies die Zeitung!*	*Lee el periódico*

With instructions of any kind it is possible to get the children off their seats for five or ten minutes of action and fun. The basic classroom language list above could be used to start a team game where the children have to carry out your instructions for real, for example:

Ferme la fenêtre, ouvre la porte, ramasse les cartes/les jouets, danse avec moi, etc.

And you can then turn the tables on the children and get them to come out and be the teacher, giving their own instructions. Eventually this could be turned into a game of charades where the teams have to guess the action and say it in the new language.

» Pupil Talk at KS2 – their 'survival kit'

If the new language is eventually to become the 'normal' medium for interaction between you and your pupils and from pupil to pupil, the children will need to learn key phrases and expressions over the four years of KS2 to cope with a range of everyday classroom situations. The language your pupils will need falls into two distinct categories:
  • The 'survival kit' they will need to communicate with you on an individual basis – pupil/teacher interaction.
  • The language they will need to play games in groups/pairs or to practise dialogues and role-plays with a partner – pupil/pupil interaction.

For their survival kit they will need to learn phrases to interact with you and ask you questions:

Asking for help		
Pardon, madame!	*Entschuldigen Sie, Frau X.*	*¡Por favor!*
Aidez-moi, s'il vous plaît!	*Ich brauche Hilfe!*	*¿Me ayuda(s), por favor?*
Je ne comprends pas.	*Ich verstehe nicht.*	*No entiendo.*
Asking for repetition		
Vous pouvez répéter, s'il vous plaît?	*Wiederholen Sie bitte!*	*¿Puede(s) repetir, por favor?*
Asking for clarification		
Comment dit-on en francais...?	*Wie sagt man auf deutsch ...?*	*¿Cómo se dice .....en español?*
		¿Cómo se escribe?

Asking for equipment

Je n'ai pas de feutre.	*Ich habe kein Filtz.*	*No tengo rotulador.*
J'ai perdu ma gomme.	*Ich habe meinen Radiergummi verloren.*	*He perdido mi goma.*

Asking where something is

Où est la colle, s'il vous plaît?	*Wo ist der Klebstoff bitte?*	*¿Dónde está el pegamento, por favor?*
Où sont les ciseaux?	*Wo soll ich das Bild hinlegen?*	*¿Dónde están las tijeras?*

Asking for where to put something

Où est-ce que je mets la peinture?	*Wo soll ich das Bild hinlegen?*	*¿Dónde pongo la pintura?*

Giving explanations/demonstrating

On coupe le papier comme ça.	*Man schneidet das Papier so.*	*Se corta el papel así.*
Puis on le déplie sur la ligne.	*Dann falten wir es auf der Linie.*	*Después, se dobla sobre/en la línea.*

Giving excuses

J'ai perdu le papier.	*Ich habe das Blatt verloren.*	*He perdido el papel.*

Giving directions to others

Tu colories les animaux.	*Du malst die Tiere an.*	*Tienes que colorear los animales.*
Tu les découpes.	*Du schneidest sie aus.*	*Los recortas.*
Tu les colles dans ton cahier.	*Du klebst sie in dein Heft.*	*Los pegas en el cuaderno.*

Describing people and things

Mon ami James est petit et mince.	*Mein Freund James ist klein und mager.*	*Mi amigo Jaime es pequeño/ bajito y flaco/delgado.*
Il porte un pantalon gris et un pull rouge.	*Er hat eine graue Hose und einen roten Pulli an.*	*Lleva un pantalón gris y un suéter/jersey rojo.*
Mon petit chaton Timmy a un an. Il est orange, noir et blanc.	*Meine Katze Mitzi ist zwei Jahre alt. Sie ist orange, schwarz und weiß.*	*Mi gatito Timmy tiene un año. Es de color canela, negro y blanco.*

Expressing likes and dislikes		
Moi, j'aime bien les glaces.	*Ich esse gern Eis.*	*Me gustan los helados.*
J'adore le foot.	*Ich spiele sehr gern Fußball.*	*Me encanta el fútbol*
Je n'aime pas les haricots – je préfère les carottes.	*Bohnen mag ich nicht - ich esse lieber Karotten.*	*No me gustan las judías. Prefiero las zanahorias.*
Je déteste les pommes frites.	*Schnecken mag ich gar nicht.*	*No me gustan nada las patatas fritas.*

» Pupil/pupil language in the active classroom

If you are to create a really active classroom in which the pupils are just as involved as you are, you will need to devise a range of activities that require the pupils to speak to each other, not just to you.

Pairwork and role play, team games, board and card games need to become regular features of your lessons. But these pupil/pupil activities will not succeed unless you first teach the children the phrases they will need to interact with each other in the new language. If you fail to do this, the children will inevitably drop back into English the moment your back is turned.

Role playing language

Role playing language		
Tu es A, je suis B.	*Du bist A, ich bin B.*	*Tu eres A, yo soy B.*
Tu commences/ je commence.	*Du beginnst/ich beginne.*	*Empiezas tú, empiezo yo.*
C'est à toi.	*Du bist dran.*	*Te toca a ti.*
Madame/ Maîtresse, nous avons fini!	*Frau X, wir sind fertig!*	*¡Hemos terminado!*
Game-playing language		
C'est à moi.	*Ich bin dran.*	*Me toca a mí.*
C'est mon/ton tour.	*Jetzt komme ich/kommst du dran.*	*Es mi turno (?)*
Paul, tu as Monsieur B le boulanger?	*Paul, hast du Herrn B, den Bäcker?*	*Paul, ¿tienes al Sr. B, el panadero?*
Attends! Un moment!	*Moment mal! Warte!*	*¡Espera! ¡Un momento!*

Tu triches! Ne triche pas!	Du mogelst! Nicht schwindeln!	Estás haciendo trampa. No hagas trampa.
Avance/recule de 2 cases.	2 Felder vorwärts/zurück.	Adelanta/retrocede dos casillas.
Passe un tour.	Einmal aussetzen.	Pierdes un turno.

You will find an extensive repertoire of phrases, mainly in French and some in German, for playing games of all kinds in *Games and fun activities* (YPF2); in *Let's join in!* (YPF6) and in the CILT Resource File 2: *Rhythm and Rhyme*.

Many of these phrases could be introduced in a game: *à moi/à toi* could be taught by taking turns to throw a softball to each other; *j'avance/je recule* could be taught on a hopscotch court with the children jumping forward/back to specific squares. Other phrases could be introduced to the class by playing a demonstration game with your classroom assistant, your FLA (if you are lucky enough to have one) or with one pupil. Once the demonstration game has been played, you will need to find some way of providing the children with visual support if they are to use the phrases among themselves – wall display or phrase cards. You will certainly have to rehearse the phrases with the class – adding gestures/body language where possible until you are satisfied that they can pronounce them properly.

Remember that your Foreign Language Assistant (FLA) can play a vital role here by circulating from table to table, prompting, encouraging, and checking that each group is using the correct phrases and pronunciation.

» Total physical response (TPR)

The teaching and learning of new vocabulary can be greatly enhanced if your pupils are encouraged to move physically in response to instructions, descriptions and stories told in the new language. TPR helps the children to fix the new phrases in their memories and such action songs as 'Head and shoulders, knees and toes', *'Alouette'* or the 'Hokey-cokey' or the game of 'Simon says' are well-tried examples.

The technique can be transferred to all sorts of classroom situations: when learning classroom instructions, the class can play team games where they have to race to carry out the task:

Ferme la porte!	Mach dir Tür zu!	Cierra la puerta
Ouvre la fenêtre!	Mach das Fenster auf!	Abre la ventana
Allume la lumière!.	Mach das Licht an!	Enciende la luz
Essuie le tableau!	Wisch die Tafel ab!	Limpia la mesa

You can adapt many party games to have teams competing:

Apporte-moi une trousse/un crayon/une gomme.

Bring mir einen Radierer/einen Bleistiftspitzer einen Kugelschreiber.

You can devise nonsense games where you challenge the class to carry out your instructions:

Pose ton cahier sur ta chaise.	*Leg dein Heft auf deinen Stuhl.*
Pose ta gomme sur le cahier,	*Leg deinen Radiergummi auf das Heft.*
Assieds-toi!	*Setz dich hin!*
Pose ton crayon sur ta tête,	*Leg deinen Bleistift auf deinen Kopf.*
Lève la main gauche,	*Heb die linke Hand.*
Touche ton pied droit,	*Greif deinen rechten Fuß an.*

Another way of using TPR is to invite pupils to stand up, clap or mime in response to your questions:

Si tu aimes les bananas/les glaces, mange une! (Mime)	*Wenn du gern Eis/Bananen ißt, iß eins/eine!* (Mime)	*Si te gustan los plátanos/los helados, cómete uno*
Si tu sais nager/faire du vélo, montre-nous!	*Wenn du schwimmen/ radfahren kannst, zeig uns!*	*Si sabes nadar/montar en bici, enséñanos*
Si tu as des frères, bats les mains/claque les doigts!	*Wenn du Brüder hast, klatsch in die Hände/ schnips mit den Fingern!*	*Si tienes hermanos, da palmadas/chasquea los dedos*
Si c'est ton anniversaire aujourd'hui/cette semaine, lève-toi!	*Wenn du heute/diese Woche Geburtstag hast, steh auf!*	*Si hoy/esta semana es tu cumpleaños, levántate*

TPR can equally well be applied to story-telling. A story like *Goldilocks, The very hungry caterpillar*, or *The enormous turnip* told in a simplified version in the new language, can be introduced using big books with large visuals of the main characters, events or places on the whiteboard and the children can be invited to invent their own mimes to accompany each character or event. Each time they hear them as you narrate the story, the children mime the action and are thus drawn into the story even though they do not understand every word. An example from Goldilocks might be:

Boucle d'Or pousse la porte et entre sur la pointe des pieds. (Children mime)
Elle a faim.
Elle goûte la soupe d'une grande assiette. Aïe, c'est chaud!
Quelqu'un a goûté ma soupe, dit le gros ours.
Quelqu'un est couché dans mon lit, dit le petit ours.

A whole range of ideas for story-telling can be found in *Are you sitting comfortably?* (YPF3).

Further ideas for TPR activities are always to be found in EFL materials such as Susan Halliwell's *Teaching English in the Primary Classroom* and in Sarah Phillips's *Young Learners*.

» Puppets

Whether you are starting with a KS1 or KS2 class you will not find a better motivator or a better ally in the classroom than a big cuddly puppet (or a big furry animal with presence!).

A puppet rarely fails to catch the imagination of small children – even ten-year-olds – and he/she becomes the focus of attention for minutes on end. Shy children will usually come out of their shell to relate to a new, non-threatening personality in the classroom. So why are puppets so useful in teaching languages?

Puppets are irresistible – you can shake hands with them, kiss them, hug them, play jokes on them!

A puppet can adopt all sorts of characteristics, depending on the teacher's histrionic talents and imagination. First of all it must have a name: preferably a name typical of the new language.

A puppet can:
- talk to the teacher;
- talk to the whole class;
- talk to and touch individual children;
- make silly mistakes;
- get up to mischief and show off;
- be a clown/a comedian;
- be sad/happy, play tricks on the teacher or on the pupils;
- be told off by the teacher, get into scrapes of all kinds.

- always be the children's friend and confidant, whispering the answer if a pupil gets stuck;
- be the ringleader for pupil activities, showing them what to do, demonstrating how to play a new game, demonstrating how to pronounce new words;
- show the class how to spell or write words – and sometimes getting it wrong!

In short, the puppet becomes the teacher's stooge – and of course the golden rule is that **the puppet never, ever speaks a word of English**!

If you are lucky enough to have a FLA, get him/her to be the voice of the puppet whenever possible. (Perhaps even a new puppet that only arrives with the FLA fresh from abroad?) This will add to the range of phrases the puppet knows, but the class (and maybe the teacher!) has not heard before.

Finger puppets and large glove puppets (animals, birds, people) are obtainable from Early Start Languages and other outlets. Finger puppets are ideal for the children to practise dialogues in pairs, recite rhymes or sing songs to each other. IKEA sells sets of finger puppets, but you may prefer to show the children how to make their own out of old socks, etc.

» Introducing reading and writing at KS1 and KS2

The evidence from primary schools across Europe points to distinct advantages of relating the spoken to the printed word from quite an early stage.

Of course we should not abandon the golden rule of thorough oral practice to establish correct pronunciation and intonation **before** we show the children the new words in print. But withholding the written form of the language for too long tends to inhibit the children's natural curiosity and may well hold up the learning process.

We all need 'hooks' to hang new words and phrases on and for most children it is helpful to associate the printed word with visuals/flashcards or actions without forcing the child to rely solely on 'reading' the word. So we need to think carefully about the stimuli that will help the class to memorise new phrases and provide support on a daily basis through display.

The gradual introduction of reading captions and mini-dialogues in speech bubbles is an integral part of nearly all the primary materials produced in continental Europe.

Children are expected to recognise words in print from the outset. The issue of exposing children to the printed word and helping them to relate the spoken to the written form is dealt with very clearly by Christina Skarbek in *First steps to reading and writing* (YPF5) and you will find extensive guidance in the KS2 Framework for Languages where the progression from Year 3 to Year 6 is laid out in the Learning Objectives for Oracy and Literacy. We would hope that by Year 5 and Year 6 your class are capable of working their way through a simple magazine such as *La petite presse* (Scholastic) or a set of simple graded cartoon readers such as Rosemary Bevis's *Les monstres* (Early Start Languages) or the excellent sets of graded reading cards in *A la carte 1+2* by Thérèse Bougard and Sue Finnie (LCP). Many pupils should also be able to get a lot of pleasure out of reading well-known fables and fairytales in the *Plaisir de lire*, *Lesen leicht gemacht* and *Mis primeros cuentos* series (Eli/European Schoolbooks).

While we would not expect teachers to introduce writing in the foreign language at KS1, there may be occasions where you feel that copy-writing is appropriate – and there is certainly a strong case to be made for encouraging young children to read single words, labels and captions aloud – when they are ready and when they ask! Why should a KS1 classroom not be full of mobiles, visuals and collages **made in the new language by the children** to show what they know? And the children are bound to want to write some sort of captions or labels (see Chapter 6).

Worksheets

Simple worksheets can be devised as reinforcement at almost any stage, but you are the best judge of what is appropriate for your particular class and the level of language they can cope with. Children could be asked to copy-write and match/join familiar words to pictures of the handful of new objects they have learnt this week – as in our examples on p61.

Or they can work orally in pairs:

A is blindfolded; B holds one of the objects; A has to guess what it is.

B	*Qu'est-ce que c'est?*	*Was habe ich in der Hand?*	*¿Qué es esto?*
A	*C'est une gomme?*	*Ist es ein Radiergummi?*	*¿Es una goma?*
B	*Non.*	*Nein.*	*No.*
A	*C'est une trousse?*	*Ist es eine Federtasche?*	*¿Es un estuche?*
B	*Oui.*	*Ja.*	*Sí.*

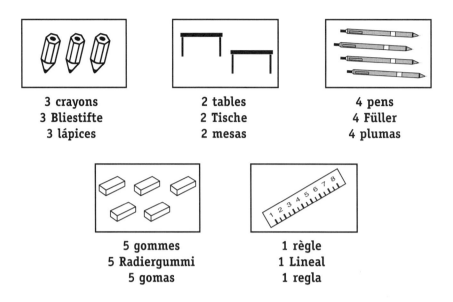

3 crayons	2 tables	4 pens
3 Bliestifte	2 Tische	4 Füller
3 lápices	2 mesas	4 plumas

5 gommes	1 règle
5 Radiergummi	1 Lineal
5 gomas	1 regla

You will have your own ideas of the kind of worksheets that appeal to your particular class, and they can be devised in the new language based on what your pupils can do in other areas of the curriculum. Clare Cooke's wide ranging sets of games and worksheets. *Jeux faciles*, *Juegos faciles* and *Superspiele* (see Resources list, p137) contain a fund of excellent ideas for primary children. There are two sets of worksheets for each language and all are very accessible to KS2 pupils.

Once you have acquired a small stock of simple new language rubrics and instructions for worksheets you can cover most eventualities. For example:

	Cherche Wally/les animaux/monsieur X	*Suche Wally/die Tiere/ Herrn X*	*Busca a Wally/los animales/al Sr. X*
	Trouve les mots cachés	*Suche die versteckten Wörter*	*Busca las palabras escondidas*
	Ecris la liste	*Schreib die Liste*	*Escribe la relación*
	Où est le fantôme?	*Wo ist der Geist?*	*¿Dónde está el fantasma?*
	Qui est-ce?	*Wer ist das?*	*¿Quién es?*

	Regarde le plan/l'image	*Sieh dir den Plan/das Bild an*	*Mira el plano/el dibujo/ la imagen*
	Colorie (l'arc-en-ciel, les animaux)	*Male (den Regenbogen/ die Tiere) an*	*Colorea el arco iris/los animales*
	Dessine	*Zeichne*	*Dibuja*
	Découpe l'image	*Schneide das Bild aus*	*Recorte el dibujo/la imagen*
	Relie (les mots et les images)	*Verbinde (Wort mit Bild)*	*Relaciona (las palabras con los imágenes*
	Complète les images/les boîtes	*Ergänze die Bilder/die Felder*	*Rellena las casillas*
	Coupe	*Schneide*	*Recorta*
	Plie	*Falte*	*Dobla*
	Colle	*Klebe*	*Pega*
	Attache	*Hefte*	*Junta*

	Relie:	Verbinde:	Relaciona:
	une tortue	*eine Schildkröte*	*Una Tortuga*
	un éléphant	*ein Elefant*	*Un elefante*

	un chien	ein Fisch	un perro
	un poisson	ein Schwein	un pez
	un cochon	ein Hund	un cerdo
	un chat	eine Schlange	un gato
	un serpent	ein Kaninchen	una serpiente
	un lapin	eine Katze	un conejo

Dessine et colorie
Zeichne und male an
Dibujar y color

un chat noir
eine schwarze Katze
Un gato negro

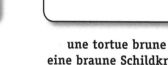

une tortue brune
eine braune Schildkröte
Una tortuga marrón

un serpent vert
eine grüne Schlange
Una serpiente verde

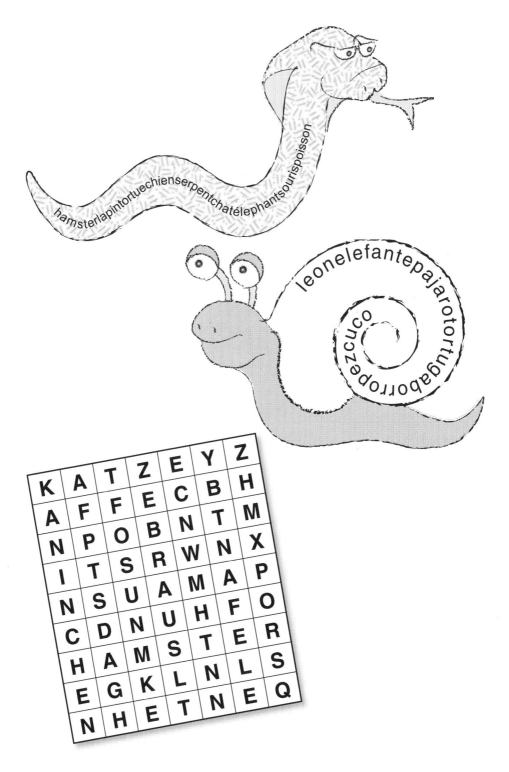

hamsterlapintortuechienserpentchatélephantsourispoisson

leonelefantepajarotortugaborropezcuco

K	A	T	Z	E	Y	Z
A	F	F	E	C	B	H
N	P	O	B	N	T	M
I	T	S	R	W	N	X
N	S	U	A	M	A	P
C	D	N	U	H	F	O
H	A	M	S	T	E	R
E	G	K	L	N	L	S
N	H	E	T	N	E	Q

» Lesson planning

To conclude this chapter we would like to draw your attention to the wide range of helpful advice now available in print and via the internet. If you are looking for down -to-earth basic advice on lesson planning, you could find no better starting point than the ideas set out on pp17–19 of the *Teachers' guide* to the QCA Schemes of Work at KS2. Here you will find suggestions for a teaching sequence of **presentation >> practice >> production**.

This approach provides a sequence of activities that takes children from their first encounter with new words and phrases (the presentation stage), through a series of games and activities to **practise** and **consolidate** the new language items, building confidence and familiarity with words in sound and print, and finally on to the **performance stage** where the children are encouraged to use the language for real – in their own way and for their own purposes.

If you are looking for inspiration to see how this is done in the classroom in your language, you have only to refer to **www.primarylanguages.org.uk** where you can view clips from a wide range of language lessons in six languages in primary schools across the UK at KS1 and KS2.

Chapter 4
» Progression

Whether you are starting at KS1 or KS2 it is crucial that your school develops its own scheme of work that ensures progression in each year and across the four years of KS2. You will need a coherent learning programme that takes children from square one to a point where they can use and apply a limited, clearly defined range of the new language with confidence to achieve specific tasks that are motivating and of real interest to them. It is important that by the time they move on to secondary school they know what they know in the language(s) they have learnt with you in primary school.

They should all have made progress in knowledge and skills, in self-confidence, in learning how to learn a language, using reference skills, accessing foreign language websites and beginning to use the language(s) creatively for their own purposes – a significant step in their own personal development.

The table below illustrates how the learning of a new language helps to develop children's personalities – not just their language skills.

Progression in learning and personal development

KS1	KS2
Linguistic development	
First tentative encounter with FL:	Dialogues with a puppet.
Listen and repeat;	Dialogues with a partner.
Listen and join in- song/rhyme;	Dialogues with a native speaker.
Listen and do.	Use of descriptive language.

KS1	KS2
Mimicry – playing with language.	Progress from single words>phrases>sentences.
	Read dialogues and short texts.
	Give a short presentation in the new language.
	Cope with authentic, unpredictable texts.
	Receive/send emails/letters to pen-pals abroad.
	Increased accuracy in pronunciation and writing. First visit abroad – using the new language in real context.

Knowledge about language

KS1	KS2
Listen and understand: instructions/praise/reprimands.	Compare the new language with first language.
Read and understand captions/speech bubbles.	Look for language patterns.
	Awareness of structure/how language works.
	Linking spoken and written forms.
	Understand a range of text types:
	fiction, poetry, description, information.
	Develop ability to predict meanings; to use learnt phrases in new contexts.

Language learning strategies

KS1	KS2
Memorising: numbers, rhymes songs, mini-dialogues.	Memorising: phrases, spellings.
	Using dictionary skills: sorting and ordering; finding new words, genders.
	Using a picture dictionary > a bilingual dictionary.
	Reading for pleasure and information.
	Accessing new language children's websites for fun/for information.

Intercultural understanding

KS1	KS2
Learn about children abroad and compare own interests with those of peers.	Learners can communicate with peers in another country (e-pals/pen-pals).
	Can read simple children's magazines, stories, children's websites.
	Can make first visit to foreign country.

KS1	KS2
Self-confidence	
Can take part in mini-dialogues with puppet/partner in class – with teacher support and encouragement.	Can perform in the new language: poems, songs, drama to an audience of peers/parents.
	Can read for information and pleasure.
	Can communicate with native speakers.
Personal development	
Tentative child, tentative learner	Confident child, confident learner with skills; more rounded personality with greater language awareness in mother tongue and new language, positive attitude to language learning, ability to use a range of learning strategies.
	Self-confidence to function in a multilingual/multicultural world – at school and in the community.

» Framework for Languages

Part 3 of the KS Framework for Languages sets out in Section 5 (pp65–83) a more detailed description of the kind of progression we should be aiming at over the four years of KS2. It includes the following:

- An increasing confidence in children's understanding and use of the new language; e.g. they begin to create their own sentences and dialogues.
- An increase in the amount and complexity of language the children can understand and use; e.g. from simple controlled beginnings they can eventually tackle longer sentences/short paragraphs including authentic language from a penfriend/e-pal in a partner school.
- An increased speed and fluency of response in the new language; e.g. children can give quick answers in the new language because they are confident and secure – numbers, mental arithmetic, colours, talking about themselves, asking as well as answering questions.
- An increased ability to reuse the language in different contexts/topics; e.g. they can recycle phrases they learnt to describe a puppet to talk about their friends and family.
- Growing confidence in dealing with unpredictable language; e.g. they can work out messages from e-pals, respond to questions from a native speaker – even though they don't understand every word.
- New insights into how language works; e.g. they become aware of the 'mechanics' of languages – that sentences conform to certain patterns, that

word order can be different, that verbs, nouns, adjectives behave differently in each language.

- Increased confidence in deducing meaning by using grammatical knowledge; e.g. they can work out the meaning of a message or description through their knowledge of verb forms and the way adjectives are used in the new language.
- Developing independence in language learning and use across the range of skills; e.g. children are able to create their own questions, dialogues, descriptions by using reference skills without constant teacher support – they are able to take risks in the new language.
- An increase in range and frequency of the children's use of language learning strategies; e.g. they have acquired tricks to memorise and help them recall known phrases.
- A growing understanding of their own culture and those of others; e.g. children begin to compare and contrast aspects of their own culture with those of their peers in the foreign country – mealtimes, school day, celebrations.

In order to ensure real and measurable progress by all your pupils you will need to devise, or adapt, **a structured scheme of work for yourself** in which there is a sequence of activities which build on prior learning, ensuring that key phrases learnt at the beginning of the year are constantly revisited and recycled in later units so that the pupils do not forget them.

» The QCA Schemes of Work for French, German and Spanish

The QCA Schemes of Work are a really useful starting point – and you can adapt and amend them to suit your own needs as you become more confident. There are also free schemes of work on the Grids for Learning websites and on the Primary Languages website.

You should try to build into your programme some measurable 'waystages' – events that demonstrate to the learners and their parents that they really have achieved something worthwhile and that they can use the language they have learnt. The most rewarding are opportunities to perform in the language: whether it be a poem or a rap, a concert of songs and dances from the new language country, acting out their own version of a well-known tale, a simple playlet that they have created with costumes and props. The children will enter into the performance with enthusiasm – and these will be the events that they will remember later in life.

There is also plenty of scope for them to celebrate their language achievements in other forms: they can display collages, models and artwork labelled in the language; cartoon characters and puppets from foreign language stories they have heard or read can appear all round the school, and multilingual signposts can be created to show visitors round the school (see Chapter 5).

We discuss in Chapter 6 the possibilities for recording pupil achievement and for **informal** teacher assessment using the European Languages Portfolio (ELP) and the new Languages Ladder (LL).

By sitting down to plan your new language activities and scripting the key phrases that you wish to teach the children to use themselves as well as the ones you want them to understand, you will quickly identify your own strengths and weaknesses in the foreign language. This planning process will help you to stay in control of the language you are going to use in class and to some extent define the limits of the vocabulary you are able to use, although of course you will need to consult native speakers or someone else's scheme of work when you embark on a topic you have never taught before! The motto is to start small and gradually build up your repertoire – and the children's – as your confidence grows.

In this chapter we have attempted to show how children can progress from a gentle start at KS1 or in Year 3 to more varied and challenging work later in KS2. Under various headings we have given examples of activities well within the scope of 4–6 -year-olds, followed by activities of a slightly more sophisticated nature to challenge the 7–11 -year-olds.

Many texts (songs, rhymes, stories, on audio or video) can be used in both KS1 and KS2 – it is often simply a matter of adapting our expectations to ensure that the tasks we set are appropriate to the children's level of maturity.

» Key Stage 1

Our starting point for KS1 pupils is education of the ear – awakening the children to the sounds of a new language as described in Chapter 2.

KS1 teachers would do well to consult the Learning Objectives for Oracy as set out for Year 3 in the KS2 Framework document (see our summary of Oracy on p35), but the kind of child-centred language work you could do is well illustrated in *Entre dans la ronde* and in *La ronde des petits* (La Jolie Ronde), where Rosie Williams sets out ten simple units illustrating activities that could be covered in a term with complete beginners.

Part 3 of the KS2 Framework for Languages (Section 6, pp85–89) includes a helpful guide for teachers introducing a language at KS1; the Learning Objectives it sets out are closely linked to what will follow when children reach Year 3:

Children should be taught to:	Examples of outcomes:
0.1	
Develop listening and attention skills	– focus attention on the speaker; – make eye contact with the speaker; – look at gesture and body language of the speaker; – recognise a familiar word/phrase and give a physical response; – identify sounds in words.
0.2	
Listen with sustained concentration	– listen to simple finger rhymes, songs, stories; – watch videos/DVDs in other languages.
0.3	
Understand the conventions of turn-taking	– play circle games, passing an object round as a signal to allow children to speak; – create a Mexican wave in small groups, demonstrating one word or phrase, e.g .days, numbers, greetings.
0.4	
Copy language modelled by the teacher or another speaker	– speak in chorus, small groups, individually; – speak in a clear and audible voice.
0.5	
Sing songs and recite finger rhymes	– sing children's songs and recite rhymes in English and in other languages spoken by children in the class.

Children should be taught to:	Examples of outcomes:
IU.1	
Understand that different languages are spoken in the world	– listen to examples of languages spoken by children in the class, or teachers, teaching assistants, parents, visitors.
IU.2	
Celebrate and value plurilingualism	– be inquisitive about languages; – showcase language skills and experiences in assemblies/ presentations to parents.
IU.3	
Celebrate and value cultural diversity	– learn respect for one another; – foster attitudes of fairness, tolerance and forgiveness.

» Listening

The receptive listening skills will need to be built up until the children feel confident enough to produce words and phrases in the new language themselves. The more often we can expose them to the new language the better, so no opportunity should be missed – even if it is only five or ten minutes a day. Call the register, carry out daily routines, play/sing a song or repeat a rhyme whenever you can.

» Speaking

Productive speaking skills come slowly; initially you will not elicit from the children much more than one word answers: *oui, non/ja, nein/si, non* or simply the name of the object or person: *chat, Katze, gato* are all that we should expect from some children. You might then progress to short phrase answers:

Je m'appelle Jack.	*Ich heiße Jack.*	*Me llamo Jack.*
(J'ai) six ans.	*(Ich bin) sechs (Jahre alt.)*	*Tienen seis anos.*
(J'ai) un chat.	*(Ich habe) eine Katze.*	*Tienen un gato.*

And then you can gradually build up more phrases that enable the children to feel they are beginning a real dialogue with you:

J'habite à …	*Ich wohne in …*	*Vivo en...*
J'ai deux soeurs et un frère.	*Ich habe zwei Schwestern und einen Bruder.*	*Tengo dos hermanas y un hermano*
Mon frère s'appelle...	*Mein Bruder heißt …*	*Mi hermano se llama...*
Mon chien s'appelle...	*Mein Hund heißt...*	*Mi perro se llama...*
Il est noir.	*Er ist schwarz...*	*Es negro...*

Simultaneously with word recognition (animals, colours, days, months, etc) we need to build up the children's repertoire of **productive phrases** that enable them to communicate in the new language in class, with you and with each other. The gradual enhancement of classroom interaction needs to be a deliberate part of our strategy and this can be done only if we consciously choose the building blocks of language we want the children to learn to use for themselves. At KS1 we shall need only DUPLO bricks, but at KS2 we have to introduce our learners to the more detailed, more intricate Lego bricks of language and teach them how to construct meanings with them.

» Progression to productive skills

At KS1 most of your work will revolve round child-centred topics: me, animals, colours, shapes, cuddly toys of all kinds, simple numbers, days of the week, parts of the body and actions, simple games, etc.

Most of these topics will involve **presentation** using toys, flashcards and visuals, followed by lots of **practice** – repetition and consolidation, lots of singing, saying rhymes, miming the actions. Only you the teacher can judge when individual pupils have gained the confidence to start **producing** the language for themselves; many children signal this by mimicking you and joining in spontaneously.

Once the children are familiar with the basic vocabulary you can slowly progress to adding descriptors and putting adjectives with nouns:

Oui, c'est un serpent! Il est vert ou jaune? Vert.

Voilà mon chien? De quelle couleur est-il? Noir ...et blanc. Oui, c'est ça!

At KS2, with an increase in general learning skills, the tasks we set for Years 3–6 can be made progressively more challenging to include all four language skills: Listening, Speaking, Reading, Writing.

Receptive **listening skills** can be expanded with more sophisticated story-telling, sometimes by the teacher, sometimes by a native speaker; and we should progressively increase the range of native speaker voices on audio and video.

Reading skills can be gently introduced at KS1 (words, labels, captions) and can be built up through KS2 so that the children learn to relate the spoken to the printed word. They should progress from words, short phrases, sentences to simple cartoon stories that they can read for pleasure at their own speed. By the age of ten most primary pupils should be able to read emails and letters from penpals, short articles in children's magazines and on foreign websites designed for children such as **http://fr.uptoten.com** or **http://kidsweb.de** and be able to compile a simple newsletter to exchange information about their school and local area with a partner school abroad.

The productive **skill of speaking** can be extended by simple tasks involving longer sentences, more sophisticated dialogues and role plays. The children will need to be challenged to initiate conversations themselves, encouraging them to recombine learnt phrases to make up dialogues of their own. They can ask each other questions in class surveys, for example, and note the answers graphically or in writing. You may go further to include tasks that require the children to:
- record a personal profile in speech and in writing;
- compile (over a year) a dossier: *Moi* or *Ich über mich* or *Yo* in which the pupil writes and illustrates everything s/he can about her/himself, his home, his friends, her/his home town, hobbies, pets, etc;
- produce creative and fantasy artwork with a new language text, e.g. make a 'monster' story book or a cartoon strip for younger children to read; they could use ICT to produce much of this;
- create their own card or board game with simple rules in the new language;
- prepare performances in the new language for parents, another class or school.

Or you may decide to create more sophisticated, differentiated worksheets that present a challenge to the more able at the same time as offering support and reinforcement to less able pupils in the form of puzzles, word-searches, crosswords, gap-fillers, matching text to pictures, drawing, making and doing tasks. (See Clare Cooke's *Jeux faciles*, LCP).

Establishing a link with a partner school abroad can lead to pen-friend correspondence, video and e-pal links, exchange of parcels, sharing projects and eventually to exchange visits for pupils and staff.

School links can be set up via the British Council's Global Gateways website: **www.globalgateway.org.uk**

Pen-pals can be found on the following websites:
www.momes.net
www.schulweb.net
www.chicos.net
www.epals.com
www.etwinning.net

» Progression in language, progression in tasks

In the following examples we have tried to demonstrate how simple topics first encountered at KS1 or Year 3 can be revisited in more depth later in KS2.

As is made clear in the Framework Oracy objectives (see Chapter 2), progression can be achieved not only by increasing the level of the language presented, but also by making greater demands on pupils' social and learning skills and by setting them more challenging tasks. You will find more examples on the Primary Languages website.

KS1	KS2
Parts of the body	
Simple finger rhymes: *Voici ma main, M.Pouce,* etc. Simon says: *Touchez le nez, le bras,* etc. Head and shoulders, knees and toes: *Tête, épaules, genoux et pieds.* Hokey-cokey.	PE warm-up/aerobics. Class follows instructions with actions: *Posez, levez, baissez, courez, marchez, vite, lentement, stop!* etc. Pairs play game of 'Twister': *avec la main droite touche le pied gauche,* etc.
Numbers	
Counting rhymes, songs to practise numbers 1–10. Counting games with coloured counters/ Multilink.	Playing counting games from websites: **http://auxpetitesmains.free.fr** **www.momes.net** **www.kindernetz.de** **www.chicos.net** Counting forwards to 10, then backwards. Extending numbers >31 then >100.

KS1	KS2
Numbers (cont.)	
	Mental arithmetic: simple sums.
	Learn multiplication tables: x2, x3, x4, x5.
	Set progressively more challenging calculations for rapid fire mental arithmetic sessions.
	Children carry out class surveys (food, hobbies, pets) and present results in graph form.
	Class sets up village shop with prices (fruit/veg) in Euros, weights in kilos/grams.
	Class measures school buildings or own house in metres to draw groundplan – areas of rooms in m2 – rooms labelled in the new language.
Food and drink	
Identify common fruits/vegetables and colours; Likes/dislikes: *Tu aimes les bananes? Non, je ne les aime pas*.	Learn mealtime vocabulary – what do you have for breakfast/lunch/tea? When? Where? Who do you eat with? Who cooks? Likes/dislikes/preferences. Compare what the French/Germans/Spanish eat – and when they have their meals. Children prepare a spoken presentation of their mealtimes, then write an account for a pen-pal letter. Compare special meals/recipes for festivals/celebrations.
Descriptions	
Children draw a clown/monster/fantasy animal and colours. Learn colours, parts of body and descriptors: *gros, petit, énorme, horrible!*	Children play card games 'Happy Families', etc. to reinforce colours, descriptors. Children describe a person (friend/family/well-known personality) using more adjectives: *gros, tout petit, mince*. Individuals prepare spoken presentation based on a photo/poster.

KS1	KS2
Descriptions (cont.)	
	Class asks a pupil questions about the person, or in a quiz has to guess who the hidden personality is.
	Pupils write a description of a favourite sports personality/popstar to send to pen-pal.
Animals and pets	
Children handle furry animals and learn their names.	Children give a detailed description of their own pets as spoken presentation.
They learn songs/rhymes about animals.	Children can present a thumbnail sketch of their pet based on a photo.
They learn to identify each animal.	They can write it in a letter to a pen-pal.
They learn to describe them.	

Songs, rhymes and games for KS1 and KS2

In the following pages we have suggested a small selection of songs, rhymes and games for each Keystage. Some are well known, others will be new to you. Our Resources list (p137) points you to more.

Counting, playing with numbers

At KS1 finger rhymes like those below offer an easy way into the sounds of the new language.

M. Pouce est dans sa maison.
Toc! Toc! Toc!
Qui est la?
C'est moi...
Chut! Je dors!

Mais... Toc! Toc! Toc!
Qui est la?
C'est moi...
Ah! Je sors!

This Swiss finger rhyme is sung to the tune of *Frère Jacques*. The children form a snail with a balled left fist resting on a flat right hand with two fingers stretched out as the feelers:

Kriecht eine Schnecke.
Kriecht eine Schnecke
den Berg hinauf,
den Berg hinauf,
und dann wieder runter,
und dann wieder runter,
auf dem Bauch, auf dem Bauch.

The cat and mouse rhyme is spoken while you make cat movements with both hands. Two fingers of one hand run up the child's arm into sleeve or collar. The last verse is whispered until *hat sie!* – the mouse is caught.

Katze Katze sucht die Maus,
sucht die Maus,
sucht die Maus.

Kleine Maus spielt gern im Haus.
Hier geht's rein,
Da geht's raus.

Leise, leise kommt die Katze,
Sieht die Maus –
und –
hat sie!

The following rhyme can be practised initially with children counting on their fingers but once they have got into the rhythm it is much more fun to have them walking round the room inventing their own actions for each line, as in our visuals.

You might prefer a finger rhyme such as:

Eins, zwei, Polizei
Drei, vier, Offizier
Fünf, sechs, alte Hex'
Sieben, acht, gute Nacht!
Neun, zehn, auf Wiederseh'n!

1, 2,
3, 4,
5, 6,
7, 8,
9, 10,

Fünf kleine Finger tanzen herum,
Der Daumen der mag nicht mehr, Ach, wie dumm!
Vier kleine Finger tanzen herum;
Der Zeigefinger will nicht mehr, Ach, wie dumm!
Drei kleine Finger tanzen herum,
Der Mittelfinger will nicht mehr, Ach, wie dumm!
Zwei kleine Finger tanzen herum,
Der Ringfinger will nicht mehr, Ach, wie dumm!
Ein kleiner Finger tanzt noch herum,
Der kleiner Finger will auch nicht mehr, Ach, wie dumm!

This well-known French song is an easy tune to learn, but the text needs a lot of practice to get it right!

1, 2, 3 j'irai dans les bois, 4, 5, 6 ceuillir des cerises, 7, 8, 9 dans mon panier neuf, 10, 11, 12 elles seront toutes rouge.

Or you may prefer a more rhythmical version like David Hicks's number rap. Someone needs to start with a good drum beat!

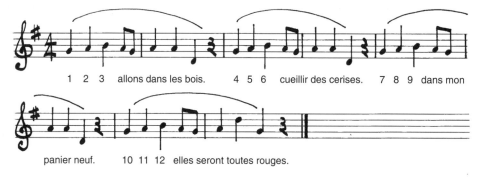

1 2 3   allons dans les bois.   4 5 6   cueillir des cerises.   7 8 9   dans mon

panier neuf.   10 11 12   elles seront toutes rouges.

1, 2, 3   *Il ne fait pas froid*
4, 5, 6   *J'adore les saucisses*
7, 8, 9   *J'ai horreur du boeuf*

The *Early Start* French, Spanish and German videos have very useful units to help teach the numbers: they teach 1–6; 7–12 and progress to simple calculations and the two times table. In later units the numbers are revisited and extended to teach 13–31, so that you can include everyone's birthdays.

There are lots of possible number games, such as 'lotto', clapping games, dominoes that match number to word, and simple snap games in pairs where the children count one or two numbers in turn:

A: *un*
B: *deux, trois*
C: *quatre, cinq*
B: *six*

and whoever says 11 (or 21, 31) first is the winner.

Simple addition and subtraction sums in the new language could be introduced for fun at quite an early stage, depending where the class has got to in maths. Children can listen to the sum in French/German/Spanish and simply pick up a number card to show you the answer:

Un et deux font 3; sechs und zwei macht 8; tres y cuatro son 7

There is plenty of scope for children to use dice or dominoes or any of the rest of the equipment available from the maths cupboard to practise saying their numbers aloud.

When children are secure with the numbers up to 20 you could progress at KS2 to playing 'Buzz' with them:

1, 2, 3, 4, *zut!* 1, 2, 3, 4, 5, 6, *Pfui!* ...8, 9 etc.

Or you can introduce regular mental arithmetic sessions in the new language, for example:

Deux plus sept; six moins trois; quatre fois cinq; dix divisé par deux.
Zwei plus sieben; sechs minus drei; viermal fünf; zehn durch zwei.
Dos y tres; diez menos cuatro; siete multiplicato por dos; doce dividido por dos.

These sessions can become quite snappy and more challenging as the children get more proficient, with numbers up to 100. Year 6 classes have proved to be quite capable of tackling teasers like:

28 + 83 − 13 = ? ; or 36 − 16 + 9 = ? and thoroughly enjoying rising to the challenge.

You could practice numbers above 20 by playing the Telephone Number game.

The class is divided into two teams; team A receives a list of the names of team B and vice versa. In turn each pupil asks someone in the opposite team for his phone number:

Team A: *Philippe, quel est ton numéro de téléphone?*
Team B: Philippe replies: 37 68 94.

All of Team A have to write down Philippe's number on their list. Then it is Team B's turn. When everyone has had a turn, the team with the most accurate transcripts is the winner.

The first time you play this game you will have to allow the class to read the numbers individually: e.g. *trois-sept-six-huit-neuf-quatre*. But when they have had some practice, they can be challenged to read out their numbers in pairs as the French, Swiss, Germans and Austrians do:

Trente-sept, soixante-huit, quatre-vingt-quatorze
Siebenunddreißig, achtundsechzig, vierundneunzig.

This is a real challenge to adults, so your class should be proud of themselves if they can manage it!

In Year 5 or Year 6 you could extend the Telephone Number game to play: 'Wrong Number'!

This time the caller A has a different number from B – he may have to ring round three or four people in his group until he finds the right connection. His mission could be to offer an invitation to a party or arrange to meet somewhere.

Falsch verbunden!
A: Hallo! Ärgerlich.
B: Wie, bitte? Wer?
A: Ärgerlich, Anna. Wer spricht denn da?
B: Hier Beckenbauer. Ist dort die Nummer: 26-87-94?
A: Nein, Sie sind falsch verbunden.
B: Oh, Entschuldigung! Wiederhören!

Vous vous êtes trompé de numéro!
A: Allo! Henry.
B: Comment? Qui est a l'appareil??
A: Henry, Thierry. C'est qui a l'appareil?
B: Ici Ballack. J'ai composé le numéro 34-75-91
A: Mais non, monsieur. Ce n'est pas le bon numéro.
B: Oh, excusez-moi, monsieur! Bonsoir!

The calendar, days, months, seasons

At KS1, you can practise the days of the week by singing them to a simple tune like the following:

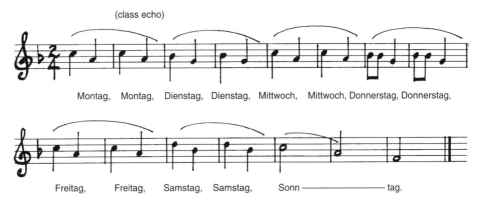

You can use the same tune for a French or Spanish version but you will have to adjust the shape and rhythm to match the different stress.

This can then be reinforced with word cards, giving the children the task of recognising the word and choosing the correct card to display each day.

At KS2, once the children have a command of the numbers to 31 you can begin to establish a daily calendar with numbers, days, months and weather symbols. Be careful to teach the date correctly:

Quel jour sommes nous? On est le jeudi quatre avril.
Eventually: C'est aujourd'hui le lundi trois mai.

In response to the question: *Der wievielte ist heute?* the children should say:

Heute ist der achte Mai, der zwanzigste April.

There are several rhymes and jingles to help the children memorise the days of the week and you can make up your own tunes to sing them.

This well-known French rhyme also has a German version:

Bonjour, Madame Lundi!	*Guten Tag, Frau Montag!*
Comment va Madame Mardi?	*Wie geht's denn Frau Dienstag?*
Très bien, Madame Mercredi.	*Ganz gut, Frau Mittwoch.*
Dites à Madame Jeudi	*Bitte sagen Sie Frau Donnerstag,*
De venir Vendredi	*Ich komme mit Frau Freitag*
Danser Samedi	*Am nächsten Samstag*
Dans la salle de Dimanche.	*Zum Kuchenessen/zum Abendessen/zum Geburtstag zu Frau Sonntag.*

Weather

At KS1, rainy weather can be celebrated with:

Regen, Regen, tropf, tropf, tropf,
fällt auf meinen Kopf, Kopf, Kopf,
fällt auf meine Beine,
Liebe Sonne scheine!

Or with:

Il pleut, il mouille,
C'est la fête à la grenouille.
Il pleut, il fait beau temps,
C'est la fête du paysan.

Both these rhymes need actions which you can make up for each line.

At KS2, at a slightly more advanced level the children could learn a rap like this one from David Hicks which introduces some French geography:

Il neige à Liège
Il fait beau à St. Malo,
Il pleut à Perigeux
Il fait froid à Blois
Il gèle à Selles
Il fait mauvais à Beauvais
Il fait chaud à Pau
Il y a du vent à Gent
Il y a du soleil à St Gervais
Il y a des nuages à Montrichard
Il y de l'orage à Paris plage
Et moi, je vais à Paris!

There is similar clapping rhyme on the CILT ELL DVD (Film 1, introduction) included in Unit 7 of the QCA scheme of work. And of course there are all the seasonal songs which have parallels in many languages. Here are two for the Spring:

Greetings and goodbyes

KS1

At KS1, when learning basic greetings, the children need to learn that body language is vital to politeness in each country: for example, shaking hands is a normal part of saying hello in many countries, especially in Germany, Austria, Switzerland, so our pupils need to learn this. The basic greetings could be displayed in class with large visuals to help them remember the meanings.

🤝	*Bonjour! Salut! Ça va?*
	Guten Morgen! GutenTag! Wie geht's?
	¡Buenos dias! ¿Que tal?

🙂	*Ça va bien, merci.*
	Danke, gut!
	Bien, gracias.

😐	*Comme ci, comme ça.*
	Es geht.
	Regular.

🙁	*Ça ne va pas.*
	Nicht so gut.
	¡Bastante mal!

👋	*Au revoir! A demain! A bientôt!*
	Auf Wiedersehen! Tschüß! Bis morgen!
	¡Adios! ¡Hasta mañana! ¡Hasta luego!

If you are prepared to sing, you could greet your class with a simple homemade jingle like this:

Bonjour! Ça va? Ça va bien, mer-ci. Comme ci, comme ça. Ça ne va pas!

Guten Morgen, wie geht's? Danke, gut! Und dir?   Es geht. Und dir?   Nicht so gut! Und dir?
¡Buenos dias! ¿Que tal? Muy bien! ¿Y tu?   Regular, ¿y tu?   Bastante mal, ¿y tu?

There are Spanish greetings songs on the Primary Languages website and in Unit 2 of *Early Start* Spanish.

Simple tunes like these cheerful Kindergarten songs could be sung every week – your class might even like to adopt one as its signature tune:

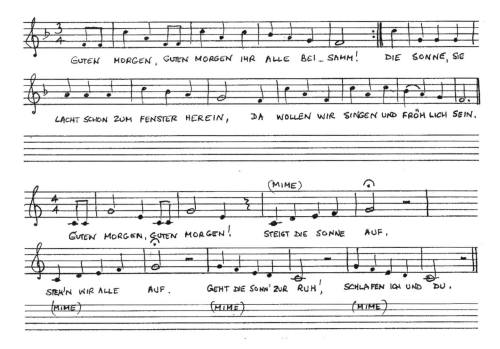

GUTEN MORGEN, GUTEN MORGEN IHR ALLE BEI_SAMM! DIE SONNE, SIE

LACHT SCHON ZUM FENSTER HEREIN, DA WOLLEN WIR SINGEN UND FRÖHLICH SEIN.

(MIME)
GUTEN MORGEN, GUTEN MORGEN! STEIGT DIE SONNE AUF.

STEH'N WIR ALLE AUF. GEHT DIE SONN' ZUR RUH', SCHLAFEN ICH UND DU.
(MIME) (MIME) (MIME)

If you want to round off a lesson with a farewell, you could teach the class:

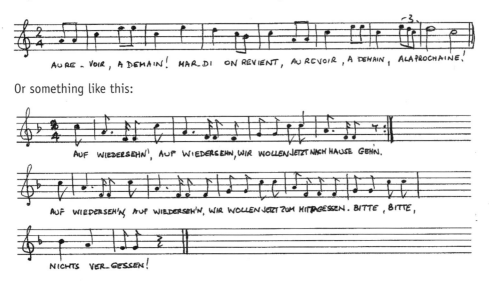

Or something like this:

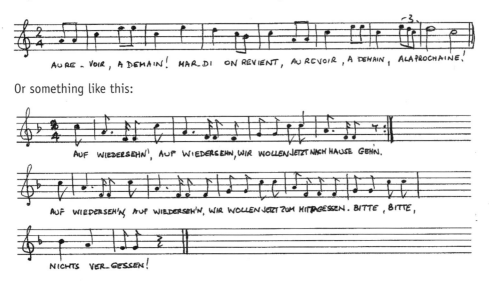

At KS2, if you wish to extend the pupils' scope for expressing personal feelings each day, your class could make their own mood thermometer like the one below:

	Einfach Klasse!/Formidable!/¡Excelente!
	Danke, prima!/Très bien, merci/Estoy muy bien, gracias.
	Danke, gut!/Ça va, merci/Bien gracias/regular.
	Danke, es geht/Comme ci, comme ça/Mal.
	Schlecht!/Ça ne va pas/Bastante mal.
	Furchtbar!/Abominable!/¡Fatal!

To this can be added expressions of surprise or sympathy – and the children can be made aware of the distinction between child/child and child/adult forms of address:

Ça va?	*Wie geht's?*	*Que tal?*
Tres bien, merci. Et toi/vous?	*Danke gut. Und dir/Ihnen?*	*Bien, gracias. Y tu/usted?*

Gradually you can add sociable phrases and ask about things that have just happened:

A la prochaine! Bon weekend!
Bonnes vacances!
Vous avez passé un bon weekend?
Où avez-vous passé les vacances?

Introductions and names

You can get young children to introduce themselves in a number of ways. You or your puppet could set the ball rolling by shaking hands and saying:

Bonjour! Je m'appelle Coco. Et toi?

Slowly the children will pick up the phrase: *Je m'appelle Charlotte*, etc. Then they need intensive practice to consolidate the greetings – perhaps through a rhyme like this:

Comment t'appelles- tu?
Je m'appelle Giselle.
Comment ça va?
Ça va, merci, ça va/Pas mal. Ça va/Oh, ça ne vas pas!

Later you might add the il and elle forms:

Comment s'appelle-t-il?   *Il s'appelle Michel.*
Comment s'appelle-t-elle?   *Elle s'appelle Rachel.*

A softball game is always a good way of getting every child to participate, or passing the parcel, the beanbag or frog will ensure that each child in turn practises the key phrases.

At KS2 the register can be made more challenging if each child has to say something in the new language, or you might enquire about absentees:

Sylvie est absente > Où est-elle?
Elle est malade/chez le dentiste/chez la directrice/chez sa grand'mère.

Wo ist Sylvia heute? Ist sie krank?
Sie ist beim Arzt/bei der Direktorin/beim Direktor/bei ihrer Oma.

¿Dónde está Silvia hoy?
Está enferma/Ha ido al dentist/está con la Directora/en casa de su abuela.

A later development involving reading and writing could be the production of a personal identity card like the ones below. These could be fun if produced on a computer with clipart to match – like the Frankenstein version.

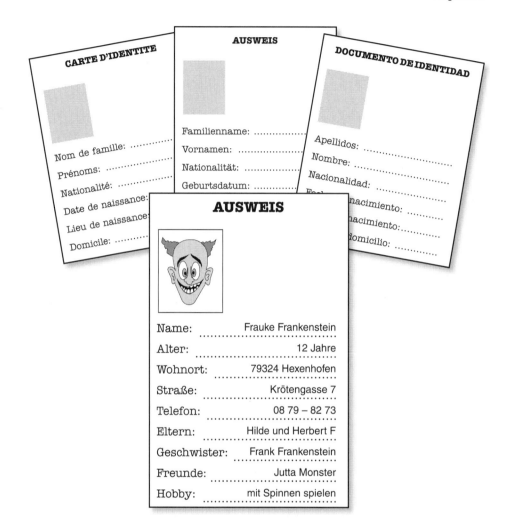

My family

At KS1 you might start with a simple rhyme like this:

J'aime papa,
J'aime maman,
Mon petit chat, mon petit chien,
Mon petit frère…
J'aime papa,
J'aime maman,
Mon petit chat, mon petit chien,
Et mon gros éléphant!

At KS2 you could offer something more challenging, like the song *Meine Familie*:

Mein Vater heißt Hans, mein Opa heißt Franz, meine Mutter heißt Renate, meine Schwester Be -

- ate. Meine Oma heißt Ottilie, das ist meine Familie. Ich heiße Fritz und mein Hund, der heißt Spitz.

Or you could get the pupils to draw their family tree, introducing parents and grandparents – though you may not wish to get tied up with dozens of aunts and uncles!

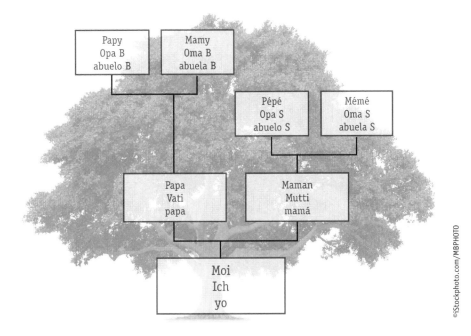

The Alphabet

At KS1, there are some very cheerful alphabet songs or chants in French, German and Spanish. You can sing the German, French and Spanish alphabet to the following tune, singing one line at a time, which the class echoes:

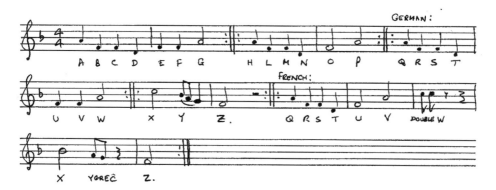

Later, in KS2, the children can be challenged to use the alphabet in speech and writing on a regular basis – they could be taught to ask:

Comment ça s'écrit? Vous pouvez épeler ça, s'il vous plaît?
Wie schreibt man das, bitte? Können Sie das bitte buchstabieren?
¿Cómo se escribe? ¿Puede/s deletrearlo, por favour?

At KS2 children could be introduced to the subtleties of pronouncing common French names like the ones that appear in your classroom resources, e.g.

[air] as in *Robert, Albert*
[aar] as in *Bernard, Gérard*
[ehn] as in *Laurence, Florence*
[aine] as in *Hélène*
[ell] as in *Isabelle, Gisèle*
[ees] as in *Alice, Béatrice*
the soft [g] as in *Serge, Roger*
[ain] as in *Kévin, Quentin, Valentin*
[ee] as in *Yves, Yvonne*
[sh] as in *Charles, Charlotte* etc.

In German you could raise awareness of the pronunciation of names like:

Ute, Ulrich, Ulrike; Jürgen, Günter and Jörg; Willi, Walter, Wolfgang;
Heidi, Heinrich, Reinhard (eye) but *Friedl, Dietrich, Dietlinde.(ee)*

Spanish requires children to hear and reproduce the 'jota' in:

Juan, Xavier, Julio, Angel;
the soft 's' in: *José, Isabel, Luisa;*
the 'tn', as in: *Lucía, Celia, César.*

A geographical information gap game could be created where each pair of pupils has an outline map of Spain, France, Germany with five place names plotted and five names missing. Pupil A has to find out from B the missing towns numbered on his/her map, and pupil B has to do likewise, both pupils writing down the town names from dictation.

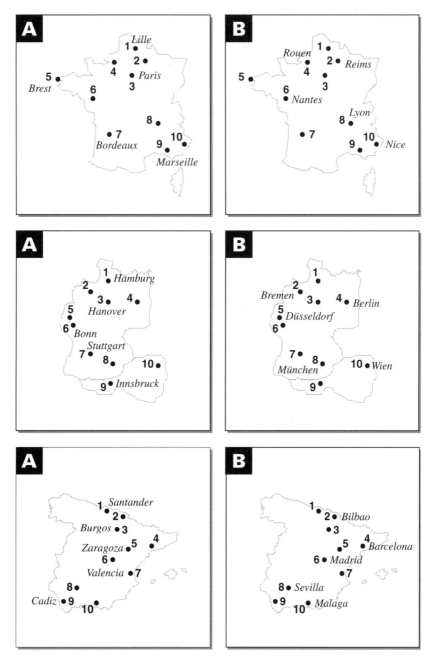

Parts of the body

To teach the parts of the body at KS1 you can use the traditional songs:

Alouette, Savez-vous planter les choux? and *Tête, épaules, genoux et pieds*. (Texts and tunes are printed in many song collections.)

The following Kindergarten song needs humorous clown actions from the teacher:

This one practices all the body parts with actions:

The Usborne *French songbook for beginners* and *Die schönsten Kinderlieder* from Ravensburg contain many of the best-known traditional songs.

The DVDs: *Voilà le Karaoké* (European Schoolbooks) and *Mon âne* (Little Linguist) add an extra visual cartoon dimension and plenty of actions. All of these can be sung with KS2 children who will soon home in on their favourites. For more modern songs with funky backing groups you will need to turn to collections like *Français, Français, Deutsch, Deutsch* and *¡Español! ¡Español!*. And don't forget that the internet also has a lot to offer. You can try **www.momes.net** (click on *école éducation*, then *musique*, then *chansons de notre enfance*); **www.kindernetz.de** provides lots of German songs and **www.yahoo.es** has Spanish songs in the section *para niños* and **www.juegosycanciones.com/splinks.html** has a wide range of songs under the section headed 'for children and their teachers'.

» Other aspects of progression

There are other aspects of progression which we cannot elaborate fully in this short book. Some schools, for example, are experimenting with teaching more than one language at KS2, as in the Language Awareness project set up in Coventry – which has a different emphasis from the single language model we have concentrated on in this book.

There are also progression issues for the many small primary schools, especially in rural counties where as many as 50% have **mixed age classes.** This raises the issue of how to cater for children in languages classes: do we offer one language in Year 3 and Year 4 and a different one in Year 5 and Year 6? Or alternate Spanish one year and German the next?

Some Local Authorities (e.g. Norfolk) are developing a 'rolling/revisiting' curriculum for primary languages in some schools. This means that teachers will need to:

- identify a limited number of key language structures and skills linked to the Year 3/4 or Year 5/6 Framework objectives;
- revisit these key structures/skills each year but in different contexts/themes;
- expect **returning** pupils to develop increasing **confidence, understanding** and **complexity** in particular when asking and answering questions;
- express expectations for **new** pupils and **returning** pupils in terms of the Framework Objectives.

This would mean that **new** pupils develop skills at a lower Framework level, e.g. single word or phrase level, while **returning** pupils would develop skills at the next level: phrase>sentence>text – and focus on questioning skills.

Once the KS2 languages programme has been running for four years in all primary schools, we shall learn by experience which models of provision work best in each area and which programmes are most rewarding for pupils and teachers.

» A footnote on music, rhythm and dance

We have mentioned a lot of songs/rhymes/singing games in this book. Music and movement contribute to the multi-sensory learning that should be an integral part of primary language lessons. As David Hicks has often pointed out, music creates a motivating environment for language learning; children access the text of a song or rap through enjoyment, musical pulse and movement. The main focus is on the music, the activity (dancing, tapping your feet, beating a drum) is paramount and the words of the lyrics are acquired by indirect learning. The music and rhythm patterns help to carry the learning because the whole body is engaged. Music and movement help learners to feel 'I can do this' – it helps to bring learners into a receptive state where their brain is relaxed; they are awake, their mind is clear and they are eager to participate.

Even a modicum of musical talent in the teacher will go a long way in a primary classroom (just three basic chords strummed on a guitar can be really useful!). But if you really cannot sing, then get one of your musical colleagues/a classroom assistant/a parent/your FLA to help – or use the many CDs and DVDs that are now available.

In any primary class there are bound to be a handful of children who are musically talented – all you have to do is ferret them out and use them to lead the singing!

There are three main categories of music available to you: made-up songs, traditional songs and modern songs for children.

Made-up songs
Songs with texts specially designed to practise over and over again specific sounds or phrases in the new language. Most of these have been made up by other people using tunes already well-known to the children – e.g. *Frère Jacques*, *London's burning*, *Twinkle, twinkle*, *Ten green bottles*, etc.

In *Let's join in!* (YPF6) and the CILT Resource File 6 *Rhythm and Rhyme* Cynthia Martin has demonstrated admirably how much you can squeeze out of such tunes.

Traditional children's songs/folk songs
There is a huge choice of song collections from France, Spain, Germany and Austria and we have listed several in the Resources List at the end of the book. Most are on CD, and a lot on DVD. You will have to choose carefully the texts that are appropriate to your class, but most traditional children's songs have easy texts, simple tunes and are often repetitive or have a refrain (as in *Alouette*). Many of these songs lend themselves to inventing actions, which always help to make the words stick. There are versions of the 'Hokey Cokey' in most European languages, for example.

Modern songs written and composed specially for children
The repertoire is constantly expanding, but for KS2 especially you will find the songs of such writers as Henri Dès, Detlev Jöcker and Martina Schwarz very appealing. There are also raps, 'funky' songs and plenty of rhythm in such collections as *Les chansons et les raps de Monsieur X* (David Hicks, Impington Village College) and in *Français, Français*; *Español, Español*; and *Deutsch, Deutsch*. But there is one health warning: singers like Dès and Jöcker are professionals who have produced a huge range of songs for children in their own country, some with quite subtle and very rapid texts which, though appealing to native speaker children, will be too complex for our British learners. So you have to select carefully the songs that you feel will appeal to your class – the ones with slower, simpler texts and easy-to-learn tunes.

Dancing

Last but not least, dancing can have a marvellous effect on your class. If you can collaborate with your music and PE colleagues, or dance teachers in the neighbourhood, it may be possible to choreograph some simple folkdances from the foreign country and eventually perform them to parents.

Chapter 5
» Displaying the new language

The value of classroom display and the role it plays in helping to learn a new language is considerable. There are many ways at KS1 and KS2 in which you can help children to relate the sounds of the new language to the printed word from the outset and you should miss no opportunity to weave foreign language captions and phrases into your general display. Your only limitation will be space!

What we need to support children's learning is a whole battery of items linked closely to the topic we are teaching, to assist both their language and their cultural awareness.

If you are short of wall space you can always use the old trick of stringing a few metres of washing line across a corner of the room and pegging your flashcards/realia to the line – and there is always the ceiling for clouds, balloons, or whatever the children design to display new captions, phrases, texts, etc.

» The children's contribution

The responsibility for new language display can be shared between the teacher and the children. The children can be encouraged to be artistically and linguistically creative and make their contribution too. They can make very good flashcards and they might also enjoy making enlarged versions of cartoon characters in the class materials you are using – or producing their own versions on computer. They will get a lot of enjoyment out of creating collages, making displays of, say, their own pets with simple descriptions and a drawing or photograph: e.g.

©iStockphoto.com/Larisa Lofitskaya

Voici mon chaton.
Il s'appele Perky.
Il a six mois.
Il est noir et blanc.

©iStockphoto.com/Johanna Goodyear

Hier ist mein Hund, Foxi.
Er frißt gern Chappie.
Er ist zwei Jahre alt.
Er kann gut schwimmen.

They might enjoy creating their own fantasy monsters which they can draw, paint or model.

Voilà un ELELOUP
Il a trois jambes et un long museau.
Il est noir, jaune et rouge.
Il mange les champignons et les pommes frites.

» The Alphabet

The alphabet can be presented and practised in a variety of ways and you will have your own ideas. You could have a classroom frieze gradually built up a few letters a week, created by the children. The letters could be related to animals, food, or any other theme – but make sure you have a good picture dictionary to help you!

The children could be really creative in colouring and making large letters as A4 flashcards so that they can hold them up to show their letter as they sing an alphabet song like the one on p93. There are French and Spanish versions in Chapter 4.

Later in KS2 when you revise the alphabet to focus on spellings you might get your class to design some really large display letters (A3 or A2), with each letter containing drawings of five or six objects which begin with that letter, e.g. *Aprikose, Apfel, Auto, Anker, Affe, Auge; Abricot, anorak, arbre, armoire, autobus, ananas,* etc.

If a few gaps are left blank in the letter, children can add more drawings whenever they learn another new word.

You could encourage the class to collect new words in a 'pictionary box'. This is in effect a glorified card index, created and built up by the class as they learn new words. It helps them to relate the word to a picture by handling it, sorting it into alphabetical order and by colour code to its gender. Some teachers encourage their pupils to create their own personal dictionaries where they sort new words by initial letter and add a picture to illustrate the meaning. This serves as a good record of the vocabulary and phrases the children have learnt each year.

It is wise to teach the numbers initially in small groups (0–5, 6–10, 11–15 and so on) and it is obviously helpful to use every practical aid from the maths equipment in your school – number fans, Multilink, etc. You could also hang pupil-made numbers as mobiles from the ceiling or put them on double-sided domino cards.

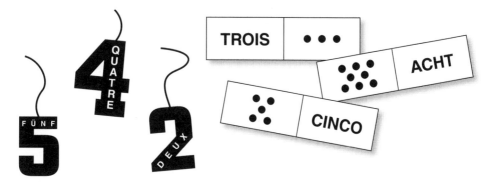

When your class is ready for it, you could make posters of the 2x, 3x, 4x, 5x tables and get the children to recite them, in the new language:

Deux fois un font deux; deux fois deux font quatre, etc.
Zweimal eins ist zwei; zweimal zwei ist vier, etc.
Uno multiplicado por dos son dos; dos multiplicado por dos son cuatro, etc.

» Birthdays

A simple cardboard poster can be made to hang on the wall when celebrating birthdays:

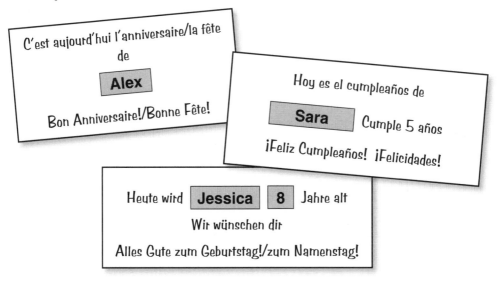

» A 'European' Corner

Whatever the age of your class there are many possibilities for making a French, German or Spanish corner in your classroom to create some 'ambience' of the countries whose language the children are learning. Here you could display realia – food packets, drinks, stamps, tickets, toys, games, photos, brochures, maps – anything that arouses the children's curiosity. The children will be only too willing to bring in realia that their family has collected on holidays abroad.

You can go further by getting the class to help you create a French/German/Spanish/ Swiss/Austrian model village or, if you have room, a shop counter which can stay in situ for a whole term. This then becomes the focus for roleplay and improvised shopping scenes; fruit and vegetables can be replaced by ice creams, clothes, shoes, etc. as required.

Plastic play money – packs of Euro coins and notes – are available from IKEA, Early Start Languages, ELC, ESB and other suppliers.

» Phrases of the Week

You may find it helps the children to memorise key phrases for classroom interaction if you display as a poster near the board three or four 'Phrases of the week'. If, for example, you have just taught them how to ask permission to do something, the list might look like this:

Excusez-moi, madame … *Je peux …* *sortir,* *aller aux toilettes,* *aller chercher mon stylo, s'il vous plaît?*	*Entschuldigen Sie, Frau X …* *Darf ich bitte …* *hinausgehen?* *auf die Toilette gehen?* *meinen Kugelschreiber holen?*

Por favor, senora/senorita
¿puedo …
ir al servicio?
ir a buscar mi bolsa?

» Classroom equipment

Many teachers ensure that everyday objects and classroom equipment are permanently labelled and colour-coded for gender:

Le téléviseur *La porte*	*der Tisch* *die Tür* *das Licht*	*la pizarra* *el armario*
Le placard *La table*	*der Schrank* *die Tafel* *das Fenster*	*la silla* *el calendario*
Le tableau *La poubelle*	*der Abfalleimer* *die Uhr* *das Brett*	*la mesa* *el mapa*

» Art and Craft

Language learning can incorporate art and craft skills if you encourage the children to design and make models based on their own experiences abroad or on video material that has been shown in class. For example, a class might make a fantasy or 'real' French/German/Spanish village or market place, including cobbled streets, market stalls, shops and buildings of various kinds, for example:

Metzgerei, Bäckerei, Tabakwaren, Postamt, Obst und Gemüse, Rathaus, etc.
Boucherie, boulangerie, tabac, poste, journaux/papeterie, mairie, etc.Carnicería, panadería,
estanco, Correos, papelería, Ayuntamiento, etc.

An excellent starting point for creating a fantasy village could be the CD-ROMs *Petit Pont* or *Kleinbrücken* (Eclipse Books) **www.manic-monkey.com**, which help children to find their way round an imaginary French/German village and get to know the shops and buildings and the characters who live there.

» Signposts

If you wish to make an impact on the whole school by showing parents and visitors what the children can do in languages, you can enlist the children's creativity by challenging them to design and make multilingual signposts (using ICT skills) to place around the school at strategic points:

You should also look for opportunities to weave the foreign language into other areas of the curriculum. Your classroom display of maths, geography, science or history could well benefit from simple captions in French/German/Spanish – or any other language spoken in the school. Collages of clothes, leaves, trees, wildlife, mini-beasts, space travel, dinosaurs, for example, could all be labelled multilingually if you think it appropriate. One-word captions may be enough in KS1 classes, but KS2 children can be encouraged to read and create longer sentences and short descriptive paragraphs.

» Children's writing

It is important that the children's artwork and their first attempts at writing should be valued by their teacher and displayed in the classroom as often as possible. The range is considerable – from simple personal profiles like our *Carte d'identité/Personalausweis/ Documento de Identidad* on p92 to family trees, which can be humorous, using a fictitious or cartoon character family as a starting point. If you think it appropriate, your pupils could then draw their own family tree and talk about it. This could be an opportunity for your class to use word-processing skills to create their own display as in our illustration:

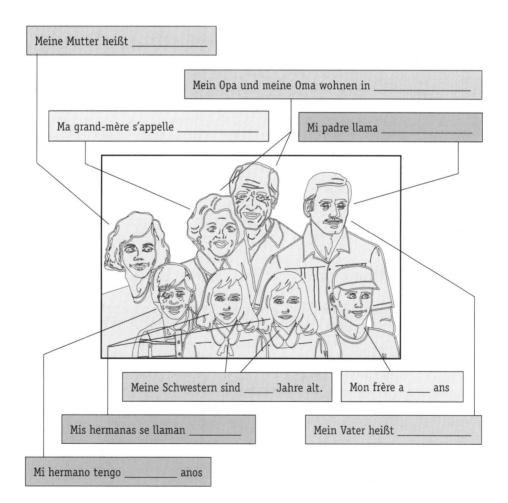

Meine Mutter heißt _____

Mein Opa und meine Oma wohnen in _____

Ma grand-mère s'appelle _____

Mi padre llama _____

Meine Schwestern sind _____ Jahre alt.

Mon frère a _____ ans

Mis hermanas se llaman _____

Mein Vater heißt _____

Mi hermano tengo _____ anos

This kind of work would be ideal for your pupils to keep in their portfolio of work if they are using the *European Languages Portfolio*. Try to make sure that when your children have produced some really good displays your headteacher celebrates their work by inviting parents to come and see what their children have done. This could be combined with an annual Languages Week when you share and celebrate all the languages that are spoken in the school.

To develop reading and writing at KS2 your class might also enjoy making up word puzzles and crosswords, perhaps for younger classes to solve. They could be wordsnakes like these:

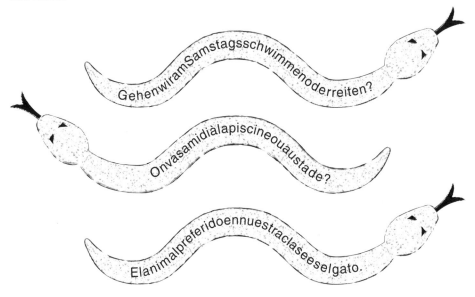

The children could be challenged to devise and display anything from simple calculations to full crosswords with pictorial clues on specific themes, e.g. animals, numbers, colours, family, games, etc. Children would also enjoy illustrating song texts and rhymes that they have learnt, for example:

Kleine Dinosaurier
spielen gern im Dreck,
dann duschen sie im Wasserfall
Und du bist weg!

Voici mon couteau
et voici ma cuillère.
Voici ma fourchette
Et voici mon assiette.
Pour boire de l'eau
Il me faut un verre.
Pour chasser les miettes,
Je prends ma serviette.

Or they might enjoy designing and making/painting mini-monsters who can talk, with speech bubbles. You will find lots more creative ideas on the children's websites we have listed in our Resources List.

» My home

After some concentrated oral work on homes, flats and houses, comparing their own with their pen-pals abroad, perhaps, you could invite your pupils to draw a sketch plan of their own home, based on a model you have provided. You could possibly download a real apartment or house plan from a Spanish or French property website with metric measurements. The challenge to draw a similar ground floor and first floor plan with their own measurements uses both mathematical and language skills.

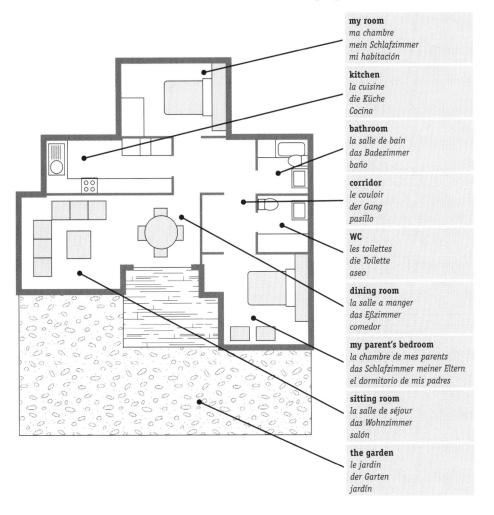

my room
ma chambre
mein Schlafzimmer
mi habitación

kitchen
la cuisine
die Küche
Cocina

bathroom
la salle de bain
das Badezimmer
baño

corridor
le couloir
der Gang
pasillo

WC
les toilettes
die Toilette
aseo

dining room
la salle a manger
das Eßzimmer
comedor

my parent's bedroom
la chambre de mes parents
das Schlafzimmer meiner Eltern
el dormitorio de mis padres

sitting room
la salle de séjour
das Wohnzimmer
salón

the garden
le jardin
der Garten
jardín

» Surveys and Graphs

Mathematical skills can be practiced in the new language through class surveys of various kinds. The children could collect data on their classmates' pets, favourite foods, drinks, ice creams, sports, or places they have visited on holiday. A survey provides an opportunity for lots of speaking and listening combined with the need to record answers and present the results in graph form. By the end of the lesson even the least confident child will have heard and asked the question at least 25 times:

Quelle est ta glace préférée?	*Welche Eissorte ißt du am liebsten?*	*¿Qué tipo de helado te gustá más?*
Tu as un animal?	*Hast du ein Haustier?*	*¿Tienes animales en casa?*
Qu'est-ce que tu aimes comme sport?	*Welchen Sport treibst du gern?*	*¿Te encantan los deportes?*

The final results can be displayed as a pie-chart or blockgraph with colour-coding:

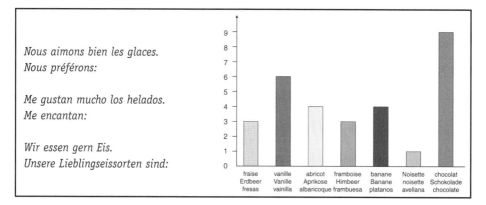

Nous aimons bien les glaces.
Nous préférons:

Me gustan mucho los helados.
Me encantan:

Wir essen gern Eis.
Unsere Lieblingseissorten sind:

» Links with a Partner School abroad

Links with a primary school abroad can lead to some of the most motivating events for the children. The arrival of a new batch of letters, emails, or a large parcel from your partner school is bound to cause excitement. The display of a selection of emails, letters, photographs and artwork creates a buzz throughout the class and attracts curiosity from the rest of the school. You can get help with setting up a link by using the British Council's Global Gateway website: **www.globalgateway.org.uk**; or visit **www.epals.com** and **www.etwinning.net**.

While it may seem premature to many teachers to attempt such a link with KS1 children, there are primary schools in the UK where children as young as six and seven have spent a week in France on reciprocal visits with a French *école maternelle*.

It is certainly an enormous eye-opener for children of eight or nine to start a correspondence with a primary class abroad and, if it can be managed, to have their first taste of a foreign culture on a short visit to the country, visiting a primary school and meeting their e-pals/penfriends. There are many such partnerships which have led to much wider exchanges of materials and joint curriculum projects involving the whole staff.

In many primary schools impressive work is displayed by KS2 pupils resulting from a residential visit to France where they have carried out a variety of cross-curricular tasks, including studies and drawings of the built environment, transects of a small town/village, town trails and historical studies. The possibilities for geographical/historical studies are endless, provided that the teachers have researched the area well and the pupils have been well prepared before the trip. Examples of this kind of assignment can be found, for example, in Fieldwork in Action 6, 'Crossing the Channel' (Geographical Association, 1998).

» Bookmaking

As pupils progress through the primary school it will be increasingly possible for them to create stories, make cartoon-strip books or short playlets of their own in the new language.

KS2 pupils would enjoy writing cartoon stories for younger children in the school. These could be handwritten with artwork, speech-bubbles, etc. or they could be word-processed and clipart added – with help from teachers or your FLA. Simple recipes could also be illustrated with artwork, for example: *La galette des rois* or *Marmorgugglhupf*. You will find recipes at sites such as: **www.fetesenfants.com** and **www.joyeuse-fete.com**.

» ICT

In the last five years the supply of good software for teaching primary languages has mushroomed quite dramatically. The development of internet websites for children in many European countries has suddenly opened up for us a wealth of authentic material that we can use in the classroom – with or without an interactive whiteboard. We have highlighted below the aspects of new language use that can be enormously enhanced by the use of the new technology, but we must refer our readers to *We have the technology!* (YPF14) where Therese Comfort and Dan Tierney take us through the potential of the internet and the interactive whiteboard. The authors show how attractive children's websites can encourage learners (and their teachers!) to explore the culture of other countries and at the same time help us to learn the language in a stimulating way, making contact with the world of primary pupils in other countries.

For teachers this offers the scope to work, even at primary level, with real websites designed for adults on, for example, weather maps/forecasts, train timetables and supermarket shopping lists.

For the pupils there is a range of sites designed especially for young children which contain:
- songs;
- rhymes and tongue-twisters;
- games;
- puzzles;
- recipes;
- things to make and do;
- pictures to paint/colour.

There are also several sites which give detailed information about festivals and celebrations in each country – and many sites are multilingual, so you just click on the language you require.

» What is the value of working with the internet?

For language teachers it opens up that world of languages that so many children have limited awareness, of and little access to, in their daily lives. For the first time primary teachers can access, at the click of a mouse, a whole gamut of authentic texts to show children that this is a real multilingual world out there. Of course you have to select your sites carefully. If you are using adult sites like shopping or timetables it is important to keep the tasks you set simple enough to suit your class.

On the other hand there are enough children's sites that your pupils will find challenging but enjoyable because the subject matter is geared to their own interests and experiences, for example:
- **www.fr.coloriage.com** (available in French, German, Spanish and Italian) could be used at KS1 as well as KS2;
- **www.fete-enfants.com** offers lots of activities relating to festivals throughout the year;
- **www.uptoten.com**, **www.teteamodeler.fr** and **http://auxpetitesmains.free. fr** offer a huge range of games and activities that primary children will find readily accessible and enjoyable to play;
- **www.bbc.co.uk/schools/primaryfrench** and **www.bbc.co.uk/schools/ primaryspanish** are two dedicated sites for primary languages from the BBC.

There is now the added bonus that you can have at your fingertips a vast resource of rhymes and songs like those we have illustrated in this book with the texts and music displayed on screen so that you can pick out new ones whenever you need them. Particularly attractive are: **www.momes.net** (click on *ecole education>musique>chansons de notre enfance*); **http://auxpetitesmains.free.fr** and the German **www.kindernetz.de.**

Chapter 6
» Rewards and assessment

» Informal rewards

We believe that it is important to reward children for their linguistic achievements on a regular basis. Success breeds success and any opportunity you can find to boost the children's confidence in speaking, reading or writing the foreign language should be seized.

In the early stages at KS1 a simple word of praise will do: *Bravo! Sehr gut! ¡Muy bien! Formidable! ¡Fantástico!* but simple rewards to individual pupils for a special effort are always good motivators and you can obtain a wide variety of stickers, stamps and small certificates in several languages from **www.superstickers.com** or **www.language-stickers.co.uk** or you can make your own.

There are many more ways of course of celebrating your pupils' achievements by display, organising festivals, celebrations and performances to parents, as we have mentioned earlier.

» Recording progress at KS2

Assessment is of course a fundamental part of teaching and learning and the KS2 Framework sets out clearly what most children should be able to do by the end of each year. It contains many examples of teaching activities that teachers can use for informal assessment. Assessment for learning strategies from other curriculum areas can be applied to language teaching and learning. At the beginning of a lesson the objective can be shared with the pupils, using language they can understand. Towards the end of the lesson teachers can discuss with pupils what they can do as a result of their learning. The Primary Languages website has a very useful section on Assessment and Recording where you can see a class involved in an 'Assessment for learning' project during a French lesson. There are also examples of peer- and self-assessment activities in a German lesson, using a simple 'Two stars and a wish sheet'.

In this short book we do not have space to elaborate on all aspects of recording and assessment, but you will find the KS2 Framework for Languages Part 3 very helpful: pp.103–114 provide examples of assessment activities, assessment for learning and setting up tasks for children's self-assessment.

There is also scope for more formal assessment throughout KS2. You can, for example, encourage the children to record their own progress by profiling what they can do in a foreign language(s) using the *European Languages Portfolio* (ELP).

The Junior version is designed to encourage young learners to record what they can do in a language, to keep examples of their own work, and make a profile of their knowledge of other languages.

The *European Language Portfolio – Junior version* consists of:
- A Languages Passport – a personalised learning diary, listing specific achievements in each of the four skills, Listening, Speaking, Reading and Writing.
- Getting Better – self-assessment sheets allowing children to assess their own competence;
- My Dossier – a file of the child's own work = a good work folder. At the end of the year the learner decides which pieces of work are to be kept.

The ELP is a great motivator and many primary and some secondary schools are already using it with enthusiasm. It is easy to manage and the children take a real pride in it. It is also a useful means of providing details of pupils' prior learning for secondary schools.

The ELP is available from CILT in loose-leaf format with a Teacher's Guide or you can download it free from the Primary Languages website.

» The Languages Ladder

Since 2006 we have a new national recognition scheme for language learners similar in many ways to the Associated Board grades for music – the Languages Ladder.

The idea of the new Languages Ladder is to provide short-term goals which are easily achievable and available to learners throughout the year. The learners can do the tests whenever they are ready. Each step of the ladder is broken down into three Grades.

Of the six steps on the ladder, the first two: Breakthrough and Preliminary are accessible to primary pupils.

The assessments in each of the four skills are informal and can be used very flexibly by teachers. The level of performance is defined by a 'can do' statement (see tables below) and pupils are not expected to reach the same grade in each skill. A Year 6 pupil, for example, might well show a performance that could be recorded like this:

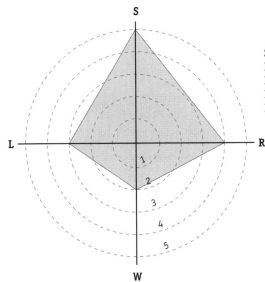

Skills profile of a child who has reached:
Level 5 (Preliminary: Grade 5) in speaking
Level 4 (Preliminary: Grade 4) in reading
Level 3 (Breakthrough: Grade 3) in listening
Level 2 (Breakthrough: Grade 2) in writing

As you can see from the Grade definitions there is nothing daunting in these assessments; they are meant to reward achievement. They are purely voluntary, as is the award of certificates – and they have nothing to do with SATs!

By the end of KS2 we would expect most pupils to achieve Grades 1–3 with ease and, in time, some pupils may well surprise us by reaching Grades 4 or 5 in Year 6.

You can find full information on the Languages Ladder at:
www.dfes.gov.uk/languages/DSP_languagesladder.cfm

External certification is also available. You can find details from Asset Languages:
www.assetlanguages.org.uk

Breakthrough: Grade 1	
Listening	I can understand a range of familiar spoken words and phrases.
Speaking	I can say/repeat a few words and short simple phrases.
Reading	I can recognise and read out a few familiar words and phrases.
Writing	I can write or copy simple words or symbols.

Breakthrough: Grade 2	
Listening	I can understand a range of familiar spoken phrases.
Speaking	I can ask and answer simple questions and give basic information.
Reading	I can understand familiar written phrases.
Writing	I can write one of two short sentences and fill the words in on a simple form.

Breakthrough: Grade 3	
Listening	I can understand the main point(s) from a short spoken message.
Speaking	I can ask and answer simple questions and talk about my life.
Reading	I can understand the main point(s) from a short written passage in clear printed script.
Writing	I can write 2–3 short sentences, using reference materials/with the support of a peer.

Preliminary: Grade 4

Listening	I can understand the main points and sone of the detail from a short spoken passage.
Speaking	I can take part in a simple conversation and I can express my opinions.
Reading	I can understand the main points and some of the detail from a short written passage.
Writing	I can write a short passage of 3–4 sentences, using reference materials/ with the support of a peer.

Preliminary: Grade 5

Listening	I can understand the main points and simple opinions (e.g. likes and dislikes) of a longer spoken passage.
Speaking	I can give a short prepared talk, on a topic of my choice, including expressing my opinions.
Reading	I can understand the main points and simple opinions (e.g. likes and dislikes) of a longer written passage.
Writing	I can write a short passage on everyday topics

Preliminary: Grade 6

Listening	I can understand spoken passages referring to past or future events.
Speaking	I can give a short prepared talk, on a topic of my choice expressing opinions and answering simple questions about it.
Reading	I can understand longer passages and distinguish present and past or future events.
Writing	I can write a simple text, e.g. a letter, giving and seeking information.

» Conclusion

We have emphasised how important it is for every primary language teacher to be familiar with the content and advice in the KS2 Framework for Languages, and there is a network of Regional Support Groups throughout England to help you with this. But remember that the Framework was designed as a 'climbing frame' for teachers not a strait-jacket! When you are dealing with a dozen different subjects in the course of the week you will not have time to refer constantly to this weighty tome once term is under way.

What you do need to have constantly to hand is your tailor-made scheme of work that helps you to plan out the new language that you and the children are going to learn together. The QCA Schemes of Work do this for you in French, German or Spanish – with all the cross-referencing to the KS2 Framework done for you – and there are several other schemes available in Local Authorities and on-line.

Don't work in isolation. Try to access local training in your own authority and plan with another like-minded colleague – and if you can find a handy native speaker (an FLA, a secondary specialist, a parent) as your language consultant, so much the better!

If it helps you to script key phrases and stick them to your desk, that is nothing to be embarrassed about – we have seen secondary teachers do the same, and we've done it ourselves! The crucial thing is to feel happy and confident with the limited amount of language you are going to use to organise the children and their learning activities.

All language teachers make mistakes from time to time – with genders, pronunciation, word order – so just wade in and have fun with the new language! If you are enjoying yourself, your enthusiasm will rub off on the children.

The clue is to make a little language go a long way. Keep your instructions short, your praise and reprimands as snappy as possible, so that the children can learn them too. A well-drilled Year 4 class, for example, should be able to mime all of your regular instructions and carry them out at the drop of a hat!

Above all, remember to make your language lessons full of lively games and activities, and then the children will learn without realising it, because they are so involved in the task.

Appendix 1
» Basic language for classroom interaction

In a book of this size it is not possible to provide a fully comprehensive list of phrases you may need one day in class. but we have attempted to offer a basic list as a starting point for non-specialist teachers covering most of the situations outlined on p10.

Note: Linguistic and/or cultural items that need special attention from the teacher are highlighted with a [g] for grammar or [c] for culture.

1 Arriving at the classroom

Rangez-vous!	Get in line, please.	*Eine Reihe, bitte!*
Vite, mettez-vous en rangs!	Line up quickly!	*Schön einreihen!*
On se met en rangs!	Queue up properly!	*Stellt euch schön an!*
		Schlange stehen, bitte!
Simon, range-toi!	Simon, get in line!	*Simon, stell dich brav an!*
Stéphanie, tu te ranges, stp.		
Taisez-vous!	Quiet, please!	*Ruhe, bitte!*
Vous vous taisez, svp.		*Seid jetzt still, bitte!*
Alain, tais-toi!	Alan, be quiet!	*Alan, sei still!*
Tu me laisses passer?	Can I come past?	*Darf ich bitte vorbei?*
Laissez-moi passer!	Let me through, please!	*Laßt mich bitte vorbei!*
Vous me laisser passer, messieurs!	Let me come past.	*Ich möchte vorbei, meine Herren!*

Entrez!	In you go!	*Geht hinein!*
Allez-y!	Go in!	*Los!*
On y va!		*Auf geht's!*
En silence, svp!	In silence, please!	*In Ruhe, bitte!*
Avancez en silence!		*Geht leise hinein!*

[g] *Vous* for the whole class/several pupils; *Tu* for individuals.
The phrases: *'s'il te plaît'* and *'s'il vous plaît'* have been abbreviated to 'stp' and 'svp' throughout these lists.

2 Greetings

Bonjour!	Good morning!	*Guten Morgen!*
Bonjour, tout le monde!		*Guten Tag! Grüß Gott!**
Ça va?	How are you all?	*Wie geht's (euch)?*
Ça va mieux, Julie?	Are you better, Julia?	*Geht's dir jetzt besser, Julia?*
Bon, asseyez-vous!	Good. Sit down please.	*Gut. Setzt euch, bitte!*
Assieds-toi vite, Ben!	Quickly, Ben — sit down!	*Ben, setz dich schnell, bitte!*

[c] French teachers do not say: *'Bonjour la classe'* or *'Bonjour les enfants!'*
These are anglicisms that should be avoided.
'Salut!' is a familiar greeting amongst friends: pupil to pupil, but not teacher to pupil nor pupil to teacher.

[c] **'Guten Tag!'* and *'Grüß Gott!'* can be used at any time of day until the evening, when you say *'Guten Abend!'*
'Grüß Gott!' is the normal greeting in Bavaria and Austria, but is not used in North Germany.
'Hallo!' is a common informal greeting among children and young people.

3   Getting settled

Qui ferme la porte?	Who is shutting the door?	*Wer macht die Tür zu?*
Bernard, tu fermes la porte, stp!	Bernard, shut the door please.	*Bernd, mach die Tür zu, bitte!*
Paul, mets la balle sous la table.	Paul, put the ball under the table.	*Paul, leg den Ball unter den Tisch!*
Tu poses la balle dans le placard/dans le coin.	Put the ball in the cupboard/in the corner.	*Du legst bitte den Ball in den Schrank/in die Ecke.*
Claire et Sylvie, arrêtez!	Claire and Sylvia stop chattering!	*Clare und Sylvia, hört jetzt auf!*
de bavarder!	Be quiet now!	*zu plaudern.*
Taisez-vous, maintenant!		*Seid endlich einmal still!*
Bon, taisez-vous!		*Seid still, bitte!*
Stéphane, un peu de calme, svp!	Stephen, let's have some quiet.	*Stefan, du sollst still sein, ja?*
Ecoutez!	Listen!	*Hört zu!*
Attention, svp!	Pay attention.	*Paßt gut auf!*

4   Calling the register

Alors, tout le monde est là?	Is everyone here?	*Also, seid ihr alle da?*
Bon, je fais l'appel. *On va faire/commence par l'appel.*	I'm calling the register.	*Wer hat das Klassenbuch, bitte?** *Gut. Ich rufe jetzt die Namen auf.*
Où sont Sandrine et Laura? *Sandrine et Laura, où sont-elles?*	Where are Sabina and Laura?	*Wo sind Sabine und Lore?* *Sind Sabine und Lore noch nicht da?*
Laura n'est pas là?	Is Laura not here?	*Lore ist nicht da?*
Où est-elle?	Where is she then?	*Wo ist sie denn?*
Stéphane est absent?	Is Sabina away?	*Stefan fehlt?*

Il est malade?	Is he ill?	Ist er krank?
Qui mange à la cantine aujourd'hui?	Who is having a school dinner today?	Wer ißt heute zu Mittag in der Kantine?
Levez la main, si vous mangez/ceux qui mangent à la cantine aujourd'hui.	Put up your hand if you are having a school meal today.	Hebt die Hand, wenn ihr heute in der Kantine eßt.
Qui déjeune à la cantine à midi?	Who is having a school dinner today?	Wer bleibt zum Mittagessen in der Schule?**

[c] *The *Klassenbuch* in Germany/Austria is not just an attendance register; it is also a record of grades (1–6) awarded to pupils by subject teachers and is usually taken by a pupil from lesson to lesson for the teacher to sign.

**School dinners are virtually unknown in most parts of Germany/Austria; most children go home to lunch between 1 and 2 o'clock — the end of the school day.

5 Organising ourselves

Pierre, assieds-toi!	Peter sit down.	Peter, setz dich!
Assieds-toi, stp Sylvain!	R/S sit down please.	Setz dich bitte Reinhard!
Je t'attends, dépêche-toi!	Hurry up, I'm waiting.	Mach schnell. Ich warte!
On vous attend, dépêchez-vous!	Quick, we're all waiting.	Schnell! Wir warten auf euch.
Alain, tu poses ton cartable, stp!	Alan put your bag down.	Alan, stell die Tasche hin, bitte!
Posez votre cartable par terre, svp.	Put all your bags on the floor.	Stellt eure Taschen hin!
Anne, tu enlèves ton manteau/ton anorak, stp!	Anne take your coat/anorak off.	Anna, zieh deinen Mantel/deinen Anorak aus!
Tout le monde est assis?	Sit down everyone.	Setzt euch jetzt!
Ça y est?	Are we ready?	Sind wir soweit?
Bon, on va commencer.	Let's begin.	Gut. Wir fangen an/wir beginnen.
Sortez vite votre cahier trousse	You need your exercise books	Ihr braucht euer Heft/eure Heft
votre trousse/votre stylo/vos crayons.	pencil case/a biro/your pencils.	Federtasche/einen Kugel-schreiber/eure Farbstifte.

| Denis, tu as ta trousse? | Dennis have you got your pencil case? | Dieter, hast du deine Federtasche? |
| Tu n'a pas de stylo? | Haven't you got a biro? | Hast du keinen Kugelschreiber? |

6 Getting attention

Bon. Taisez-vous maintenant!	Quiet now, please.	Also, Ruhe jetzt!
Paul, tais-toi donc!	Paul, stop talking,	Paul, sei doch still!
Je vous attends!	I'm waiting.	Ich warte auf dich/euch!
On t'attend, Philippe!	Philip we're all waiting for you.	Philip, wir warten alle auf dich!
Taisez-vous les autres!	The rest of you be quiet!	Hallo! Still sein, bitte!
Ça suffit!	That's enough now!	Das genügt!/Jetzt hab' ich genug!
C'est fini! C'est terminé!	Stop it!	Schluß damit! Hört jetzt auf!

7 Setting the programme for the lesson

Bon. Aujourd'hui on va...	Today we are going to...	Also, heute werden wir...
écouter la cassette.	listen to the cassette.	uns die Kassette anhören.
regarder une vidéo.	watch a video.	uns einen Video ansehen.
regarder la télé.	watch television.	fernsehen.
répéter les numéros 11 à 20.	revise the numbers 11–20.	die Nummern von 11–20 wiederholen.
chanter une chanson.	sing a song.	ein Lied singen.
apprendre un poème/une comptine.	learn a new poem/song.	ein neues Gedicht/ein neues Lied lernen.
réviser les...	revise the...	die... wiederholen

Tout d'abord on va...	First we are going to...	*Zuerst einmal wollen wir...*
Ensuite vous allez lire/	Then you will read/	*Dann werdet ihr lesen/*
écrire/dessiner...	write/draw...	*schreiben/zeichnen...*
Et enfin nous allons chanter/	And at the end we'll sing/	*Und zum Schluß wollen wir*
jouer à un jeu.	play a game.	*singen/ein Spiel machen.*

8   Starting the lesson

Bon alors, vous sortez votre trousse/votre cahier de brouillon.	Now you will need your pencil case/your rough book.	*Gut. Ihr braucht eure Federtasche/euer Notizheft.*
Vous prenez une feuille de brouillon/papier.	Take a sheet of paper.	*Ihr nehmt ein Blatt Papier.*
Vous aurez besoin devotre classeur; des ciseaux; d'un stylo feutre comme ça.	You need your folder; scissors; a felt-tip like this.	*Ihr braucht eure Mappe; eine Schere; so einen Filzstift.*
Brian, tu vas chercher les feuilles de papier, stp.	Brian, you fetch the paper, please.	*Brian, du holst uns das Papier, bitte.*
Anne, tu vas chercherles ciseaux, stp.	Anne can you bring the scissors, please?	*Anne, du bringst die Scheren, ja?*
Richard, tu donnes les cahiers/les livres, stp.	Richard you give out the exercise books.	*Richard, du teilst bitte die Hefte aus.*
Vous avez tout ce qu'il vous faut?	Have you got everything?	*Habt ihr jetzt alles?*
Bon. On va commencer.	Good. Let's begin.	*Na gut. Also fangen wir an.*
On commence par l'exercice 2 à la page 7.	We'll start with exercise 2 on page 7.	*Wir beginnen mit Aufgabe 2 auf Seite 7.*
Je vais vous montrerce qu'on va faire.	I'll show you how to do it.	*Ich zeige euch, wie das geht.*
Regardez et écoutez bien!	Watch and listen carefully.	*Schaut her und hört gut zu!*

9   Are you sitting comfortably?

Vous voyez tous le tableau/ l'écran?	Can you all see the board/ screen?	*Könnt ihr alle die Tafel/die Leinwand gut sehen?*
Philippe, viens t'asseoir à côté de Roger.	Philip, come and sit next to Roger.	*Philip, komm setz dich neben Roger.*
Qui ne voit pas bien?	Who still can't see?	*Wer kann nicht gut sehen?*
Alors, prends ta chaiseet viens ici.	Bring your chair and come here.	*Also, nimm deinen Stuhl und komm her!*

10   Discussing the date/weather

Quel date sommes-nous aujourd'hui?	What is the date today?	*Der wievielte ist heute?*
C'est mercredi?	Is it Wednesday?	*Ist heute Mittwoch?*
Quel mois sommes-nous?	Which month is it?	*Welcher Monat ist es?*
Qui peut nous dire/écrire la date?	Who can tell us/write the date for us?	*Wer kann uns das Datum sagen/schreiben?*
Et quel temps fait-il?	What is the weather like?	*Und wie ist das Wetter heute?*
Qui va changer/chercher l'image sur notre plan?	Who is going to change the weather symbol on our chart/weather house?	*Wer wechselt das Wetterbild auf unserer Wetterkarte/in unserem Wetterhäuschen?*
Qui sait la température aujourd'hui?	Who can tell us the temperature?	*Wer kann uns die Temperatur sagen?*
Lève la main si c'est ton anniversaire/ta fête aujourd'hui.	Put up your hand is it's your birthday/nameday today.	*Heb die Hand, wenn du heute Geburtstag/ Namenstag hast.*

11   Recapping

Hier/lundi/la semaine dernière...	Yesterday/on Monday/last week...	*Gestern/am Montag/letzte Woche...*
nous avons chanté...	we sang...	*haben wir... gesungen*
récité.../appris...	recited.../learnt...	*...aufgesagt/...gelernt*
joué à.../dit...	played.../said...	*...gespielt/...gesagt*

12   Presenting a new topic

Aujourd'hui /maintenant nous allons/on va...	Today/now we are going to...	*Heute/jetzt wollen wir...*
Ecoutez bien!	Listen carefully!	*Paßt gut auf! Hört zu!*
On va écouter la cassette/ regarder la vidéo/lire le poème à haute voix.	We'll listen to the cassette/ watch the video/read the poem aloud.	*Wir hören uns die Kassette an/schauen uns den Video an/lesen zusammen das Gedicht.*

13   Setting up an activity

Vous allez travailler à 2/à 3/en petits groupes de 4/5.	Work in two/threes/ groups of 4/5.	*Ihr arbeitet zu zweit/zu dritt/in Gruppen von 4/5*
Vous allez vous mettre par 3/par 4.	Get into groups of 3/4.	*Bildet Gruppen zu dritt/zu viert.*
Vous pouvez choisir votre partenaire.	Choose a partner.	*Ihr könnt einen Partner wählen.*
On va faire deux équipes: A et B.	We'll have two teams:Team A and Team B.	*Wir machen zwei Mannschaften: Team A und Team B.*
Vous travaillez tous seuls.	Work on your own today.	*Ihr arbeitet heute allein.*

14   Explaining

Vous avez compris?/vous comprenez?	Has everyone understood?	*Habt ihr verstanden? Alles OK?*
Qui n'a pas compris?	Who doesn't understand?	*Wer hat nicht verstanden?*
Lève le doigt si tu n'as pas compris.	Put your hand up if you don't understand.	*Melde dich, wenn du nicht verstehst.*
Philippe, tu as compris, hein?	Philip, do you follow?	*Philip, du hast verstanden, ja?*
Pas de problèmes?	No problems?	*Kein Problem?*
Carole, tu peux nous expliquer n anglais?/nous montrer ce qu'on va faire?	Carol, can you explain that in English?/show us how you do it?	*Carole, kannst du uns das auf Englisch erklären?/uns zeigen, wie man das macht?*
Bon, ça y est?	Good. That's it!	*Gut. So geht's, ja?*
Allez-y! Au travail!	Right. You can start.	*Fangt an. Los geht's!*
On commence. Dépêchez-vous!	Come on — hurry up!	*Ihr könnt schon beginnen. Macht schnell!*

15   Monitoring progress

Paul, c'est bien ça. Ça c'est beau/c'est joli.	That's good, Paul, very nice.	*Das ist gut, Petra. Ja, das ist sehr schön.*
C'est très bien! Excellent!	Excellent! Super!	*Prima! Ausgezeichnet!*
Le dessin est très beau.	That's a lovely picture.	*Das Bild ist sehr schön. Deine*
J'aime bien ton dessin!	I like that very much.	*Zeichnung gefällt mir gut!*
Super! Bravo! Mes félicitations!	Super! Bravo! Congratulations!	*Super! Bravo! Ich gratuliere!*
Ça c'est beaucoup mieux.	That's much better.	*Das ist viel besser.*
Regardez tout le monde! C'est super, non?	Look everyone. That's really great, isn't it?	*Schaut alle her! Das ist wirklich toll, nicht wahr?*
J et M, au travail!	J and M, get down to work.	*J und M, ihr seid heute faul!*
Il faut vous concentrer.	Pay attention/concentrate.	*Paßt doch auf!*

R, ça suffit maintenant! C'est fini!	R, that's enough of that!	R, das ist jetzt genug! Hör auf!
F, stp! Tais-toi!	F, please be quiet!	F, jetzt bist du endlich still!
X, tu n'a pas écouté ce qu'on a dit!	X you didn't listen!	X, du hast nicht aufgepaßt!

16   Explaining the rules of a game

Je vais vous expliquer comment jouer à ce jeu.	I'll show you how to play this game.	Ich sage euch, wie das geht.
Voici ce qu'on va faire.	This is how it goes...	So geht das...
Ecoutez bien!	Listen carefully!	Paßt gut auf!
La personne A commence ...	A begins...	A beginnt...
Il/Elle pose la question.	He/She asks a question.	Er/Sie stellt eine Frage.
Il/Elle jette le dé.	He/She throws the dice.	Er/Sie würfelt.
Il/Elle décrit l'image.	He/She describes the picture.	Er/Sie beschreibt das Bild.
La personne B répond...	B replies...	B antwortet...
prend une carte...	takes a card...	nimmt eine Karte...
dessine la personne.	draws the person.	zeichnet die Person.
Il faut distribuer les cartes.	You deal the cards.	Man teilt die Karten aus.
Il faut collectionner des familles.	You collect families/sets.	Man sammelt Familien/Sätze.
On va faire deux équipes de 4 garçons et 5 filles.	We form 2 teams of 4 boys and 5 girls.	Wir bilden zwei Teams mit 4 Jungen und 5 Mädchen.
Il faut former un grand cercle.	We'll form a big circle.	Wir machen einen großen Kreis.

17   Changing activity

Ecoutez! Nous allons changer d'activité.	Listen! We are going to change to something else now.	*Paßt auf! Wir machen etwas Anderes jetzt.*
Quand vous aurez fini/erminé, on va...	When you have finished we will...	*Wenn ihr fertig seid, werden wir...*
Vous arrêtez maintenant. Stop!	Stop now.	*Halt! Stop! Macht jetzt Schluß!*
On passe à autre chose...	We are going on to something new.	*Wir machen etwas Neues jetzt.*
On va chanter/réciter un poème/répéter/jouer à...	We're going to sing/say a new poem/repeat/play...	*Wir wollen singen/ein Gedicht aufsagen/ wiederholen/ ...spielen.*

18   Ending the lesson

Stop! On va s'arrêter. On arrête.	Stop! We're finishing now.	*Stop! Wir machen jetzt Schluß.*
La classe est finie.	The bell has gone.	*Es hat schon geläutet.*
Vite! Ramassez les feuilles/ cahiers/livres/ciseaux...	Quickly now, collect the sheets/exercise books/ scissors...	*Schnell. Sammelt bitte die Blätter/Hefte/Bücher/ Scheren ...ein.*
Bon. Rangez vos affaires.	Good. Pack your things away.	*Gut. Packt eure Sachen ein.*
Un peu de calme, svp!	And let's have quiet now, please!	*Und jetzt Ruhe bitte!*
Au revoir! A demain!	Goodbye! See you tomorrow!	*Auf Wiedersehen! Bis morgen!*

19   Playing games (children's phrases)

In order to be able to play simple games in pairs or small groups your pupils will need to learn a small repertoire of key phrases, otherwise they will revert to English immediately and the whole point of the activity is undermined. Here are the basics they will need and you will almost certainly have to teach them this vocabulary by demonstrating how to play each game in front of the whole class with one pupil as your guinea pig/ partner.

On y va?	Let's begin.	*Fangen wir an?*
Tu commences.	You start.	*Du beginnst.*
C'est à qui?	Whose turn is it?	*Wer ist dran?*
C'est à toi.	It's your turn.	*Du bist dran.*
C'est à moi.	It's my turn.	*Ich bin dran.*
Vas-y!	Go on!	*Mach schon!*
Donne-moi les cartes.	Give me the cards.	*Gib mir die Karten.*
Mélange les cartes.	Shuffle the cards.	*Misch die Karten.*
Distribue les cartes.	Deal the cards.	*Teil die Karten aus.*
Etale les cartes à l'envers.	Lay the cards face down.	*Leg die Karten hin mit dem Gesicht nach unten.*
Retourne deux cartes.	Turn over two cards.	*Dreh zwei Karten um.*
Prends une carte.	Take a card.	*Nimm eine Karte.*
Collectionne les paires/une série de...	Collect pairs/a set of...	*Sammel Paare/eine Reihe von...*
Combien de cartes as-tu?	How many cards have you?	*Wie viele Karten hast du?*
Pose une carte.	Put a card down.	*Leg eine Karte hin.*
Lance le dé.	Throw the dice.	*Roll den Würfel.*
Place ton pion sur une case.	Put your counter on a square.	*Leg deinen Spielstein auf ein Feld.*
Tourne la toupie.	Spin the spinner.	*Dreh den Kreisel.*
Le plateau de jeu	games board	*Das Spielbrett*
Le départ	Start	*Der Start*
L'arrivée	Finish	*Das Ziel*

Avance de deux cases.	Move forward two spaces.	*Zwei Felder vorwärts.*
Recule de trois cases.	Go back three spaces.	*Drei Felder zurück.*
Relance le dé.	Throw again.	*Noch einmal würfeln.*
Passe un tour.	Miss a turn.	*Einmal aussetzen.*
Le/la gagnant(e)	The winner.	*Der Sieger*
Suzanne a gagné.	Susi won.	*Susi hat gewonnen.*
J'ai perdu.	I lost.	*Ich habe verloren.*
J'ai gagné 15 points.	I won 15 points.	*Ich habe 15 Punkte gewonnen.*

20 Classroom objects

la porte	door	*die Tür*
la fenêtre	window	*das Fenster*
le mur	wall	*die Wand*
l'étagère	bookcase	*das Bücherregal*
le placard	cupboard	*der Schrank*
le plancher	floor	*der Fußboden*
le plafond	ceiling	*die Decke*
la table	table	*der Tisch*
la chaise	chair	*der Stuhl*
le bureau	desk	*das Pult*
le tableau	board	*die Tafel*
un essuie-tableau	boardrubber	*der Tafelwischer/Schwamm*
le chiffon	duster	*das Staubtuch*
une éponge	sponge	*der Schwamm*
la craie	chalk	*die Kreide*
le feutre	felt marker	*der Filzstift*
le magnétophone	cassette recorder	*der Kassettenrecorder*
le téléviseur	television set	*der Fernseher*

le rétroprojecteur	OHP	der Overheadprojektor
le transparent	OHT transparency	die Folie
la vidéo	video	der Videofilm
l'écran	screen	die Leinwand
le calendrier	calendar	der Kalender
le livre	book	das Buch
le cahier	exercise book	das Heft
le classeur	folder/file	die Mappe
le papier	paper	das Papier
le papier-calque	tracing paper	das Pauspapier
le papier à dessin	drawing paper	das Zeichenpapier
le carton	cardboard	der Karton
le crayon	pencil	der Bleistift
le crayon de couleur	crayon	der Buntstift
le taille-crayons	pencil sharpener	der Bleistiftspitzer
la gomme	rubber	der Radiergummi
le stylo	fountain pen	die Feder
le stylo-bille	biro	der Kugelschreiber
le feutre	felt-tip pen	der Filzstift
la règle	ruler	das Lineal
les ciseaux	scissors	die Schere
la colle (le tube)	glue (tube)	der Klebstoff (die Tube)
le scotch	sellotape	das Tesaband
le trombone	paperclip	die Heftklammer
la trousse	pencil case	die Federmappe
le cartable/le sac	schoolbag	die Schultasche

» Resources for teaching in the new language

This list was updated in January 2009. It is by no means exhaustive and you will find constant updates on the Primary Languages website.

Reading and help points for teachers

Early Language learning DVD	CILT
My Languages Portfolio (Junior ELP)	CILT
Primary Languages	**www.primarylanguages.org.uk**

Short Teachers' Guides on Primary Languages Methodology

CILT *Young Pathfinder* Series

Games and fun activities (YPF2)	Martin
Are you sitting comfortably? (YPF3)	Tierney and Dobson
First steps to reading and writing (YPF5)	Skarbek
Let's join in! (YPF6)	Martin and Cheater
Making the link (YPF7)	Tierney and Hope
A world of languages (YPF10)	Datta and Pomfrey
A flying start! (YPF11)	Satchwell and de Silva
Working together (YPF12)	Martin and Farren
Mind the gap! (YPF13)	Bevis and Gregory
We have the technology! (YPF14)	Comfort and Tierney
Speak Up! (YPF15)	Satchwell and de Silva

Leading the Way (YPF16)	Clinton and Vincent

CILT Resource File 6: *Rhythm and Rhyme*	Martin

Title	Contents	Publisher
100+ Fun ideas for practising modern foreign languages in the primary classroom: Activities for developing oracy and literacy skills.		Brilliant Publications (2007)

Linguistic upskilling

Title	Contents	Publisher
Teachers Talking French – a helping hand to fluency in KS2	Set of 6 CDs to help you learn and practise key classroom phrases	Le Petit Canard (2006)
Ici on parle français *Se habla español* *Wir sprechen Deutsch*	These books of photocopiable visuals list classroom phrases by topic covering most primary situations and include games and activities to teach the classroom language	MLG Publications (2003–7)

Visuals

Title	Contents	Publisher
Cartoons for classroom communication	photocopiable pack	MLG Publications
KS2 Picture Library	Disk of 1000+ B/W illustrations and colour pictures from Miniflashcards	MLG Publications (2007)

Classroom teaching materials

Title	Contents/Author	Publisher
Early Start French	3 DVDs + Teacher's Pack	Early Start Languages
Early Start German	2 DVDs + Teacher's Pack	Early Start Languages
Early Start Spanish	2 DVDs + Teacher's Pack	Early Start Languages
Pilote interactive: Moi; Mon école; En ville; Faisons les courses	4 CD-ROMs	KETV
Pilote interactive: Numero uno	CD-ROM	KETV
Tout le monde	Primary French Levels 1 + 2	Heinemann
Rigolo	Primary French Resource Packs 1 + 2	Nelson Thornes
Primary French is Fun 1 + 2	(interactive activities and video clips for the whiteboard)	BBC Active
Comète 1 (Y5) + 2 (Y6)	French Resources Pack	Oxford
Virtual French for KS2	CD-ROM	Collins
Boîte a Français	(Topic Boxes for KS1)	Boite à Français
Jeux de doigts	DVD + notes (KS1)	LJR
Entre dans la ronde	Teacher's Resource Book + CDs + Set of 30 suggested lesson notes (KS1)	LJR
La ronde des petits	Teacher's resource Book + CD (KS1)	LJR
Entrez dans la classe	Teacher's resource Bk + CD (Year 5/6)	LJR
Joyeux Noël!	CD (KS1 + 2)	LJR

Title	Contents/Author	Publisher
Petit Pont 1 + 2	CD-ROMs + Pupil Book	Eclipse Books/Manic Monkey
Kleinbrücken	CD-ROM + Pupil Book	Eclipse Books/Manic Monkey
Gaston 1 + 2	CD-ROM + Cassettes + Teacher's Book + Pupil's Books + Activity Book	Eli/European School Books (ESB)
Hélico! 1 + 2	CD-ROMs + Teacher's Book + Pupil's Book	Eli/ESB
Ja klar! 1 + 2	CD-ROMs + Cassettes + Pupil's Books + Teacher's Book	Eli/ESB
LCP Primary French Resource Files	Year 3/4 + Year 5/6	LCP
LCP Primary Spanish Resource Files	Year 3/4 + Year 5/6	LCP
LCP Language games pack	Horrocks	LCP
Jeux faciles 1 + 2	Cooke, Bevis	LCP
Juegos fáciles 1 + 2	Patnicroft, Cooke, Bevis	LCP
Superspiele 1 + 2	Connolly, Cooke, Bevis	LCP
Hallo, da bin ich! 1 + 2	Teacher/Pupil Books + cassettes (KS1)	Cornelsen/ESB
Tamburin 1, 2, 3	Teacher's Book, Pupil's Book, CDs, cassettes	Hueber/ESB

Songs and rhymes

Title	Contents	Publisher
Die schönsten Kinderlieder	Regensburger Buchverlag 2003	ESB
Die schönsten Kinderlieder und Kinderreime	Bassermann 2001	ESB
Hey, hey, Hallo! Learn German with a Song	Schwarz/Schulze Tamena	Goethe Institute/ESB
Detlev Jöcker Seine schönsten Lieder		Menschenkinder Verlag/ESB
Chante en français	CD with 36 songs/ poems	LJR
Canta en español	CD 37 songs/poems	LJR
Les chansons et les raps de Monsieur X		David Hicks/Impington Village College
Français! Français!	CD Funky raps and songs	The Language Factory
Deutsch! Deutsch!	CD Funky raps and songs	The Language Factory
¡Español! ¡Español!	CD Funky raps and songs	The Language Factory
Allons chanter	CD	LCP
101 comptines a mimer et a jouer avec les tout petits et les plus grands	Albaut	Bayard Jeunesse/ESB
101 poesies et comptines des quatre saisons	Albaut/Arnould	Bayard Jeunesse/ESB

Reading for children

Title	Contents/Author	Publisher
La petite Presse	Colour magazine for KS2 children (by subscription: 6 issues per year)	Eclipse/Scholastic
Galaxie	Set of graded French readers + Teacher's guide	Heinemann
L'album des monstres	Set of easy cartoon readers. Bevis	Early Start Languages
A la carte 1	Box of graded reading cards Bourdais and Finnie	LCP
Plaisir de lire – Les plus belles fables	Book + cassette	Eli/ESB
Plaisir de lire –Série Bleue	Book + cassette 5 titles	Eli/ESB
Plaisir de lire – Série Verte	Book + cassette 16 titles (well-known fairy tales)	Eli/ESB
Lesen leicht gemacht – Fabelhafte Fabeln	Book + cassette 6 titles	Eli/ESB
Lesen leicht gemacht – Die grüne Reihe	Book + cassette 16 titles (well-known fairy tales)	Eli/ESB
Mis primeros cuentos – Las fabulas fabulosas	Book + cassette 6 titles	Eli/ESB
Mis primeros cuentos - Serie Verde	Book + cassette 16 titles (Fairy tales)	Eli/ESB

Dictionaries for children

Title	Contents	Publisher
First Time French Dictionary	(KS2)	Collins
Primary French Dictionary		Chambers/Harrap
Primary Spanish Dictionary		Chambers /Harrap
Oxford Primary French Dictionary		Oxford
Oxford Primary Spanish Dictionary		Oxford
Eli Dictionnaire illustré		Eli/ESB
Mon premier dictionnaire illustré de français:	4 books: La maison/L'école/La ville/Les vacances	Eli/ESB
Eli Bildwörterbuch Deutsch		Eli/ESB
Mein erstes deutsches Wörterbuch	4 books: Zu Hause/In der Schule/In der Stadt/ Im Urlaub	Eli/ESB
First Hundred Words in French		Usborne
First Hundred Words in German		Usborne

Rewards stickers/certificates

Title	Contents	Publisher
Posters, stickers, stampers, certificates	French, German, Spanish	The Language Stickers Co.

Useful websites

For teachers

www.language-stickers.co.uk

www.superstickers.com

www.YoungLinguists.com

www.britishcouncil.org

www.globalgateway.org

www.sunderlandschools.org/mfl-sunderland/index.htm

www.primaryresources.co.uk/mfl/mfl.htm

www.teacherstv.co.uk

www.newburypark.redbridge.sch.uk/langofmonth

www.henrides.com

www.detlevjoecker.de

www.songsforteaching.com

For children

www.lcfclubs.com/babelzonenew

www.fr.coloriage.com

www.teteamodeler.fr

www.mamalisa.com/world

www.fete-enfants.com

www.momes.net

www.the-voyage.com/kids

www.joyeuse-fete.com

www.comptines.net

www.ambafrance-uk.org

http://auxpetitesmains.free.fr

www.bbc.co.uk/schools/primaryspanish

www.bbc.co.uk/schools/primaryfrench

http://fr.coloriage.com

www.navidaddigital.com

www.kindernetz.de

www.kidsweb.de

www.uptoten.com

www.quia.com

www.ecole-plus.com

Sites for children to access information

www.meteofrance.com

www.coop.ch

www.monoprix.fr

www.carrefour.fr

www.elcorteingles.es

www.kadewe.de

www.bahn.de

www.sncf.com

www.renfe.es

www.spar.at

Partner schools and e-pals

www.globalgateway.org.uk

www.schulweb.de

www.chicos.net

http://forum.momes.net/momes/Correspondants/liste_sujet-1.htm

» References

Title	Author	Publisher
KS2 Framework for Languages	DfES (2005/7)	DfES
Schemes of Work for French Y3/Y4/Y5/Y6	Cheater, C. (2005–2008)	Teaching and Learning Publications Ltd.
Schemes of Work for French Y4/5 and Y6/7	Redfearn, R. (2006)	La Jolie Ronde
Schemes of Work for Spanish Y4/5 and Y6/7	Redfearn, R. (2008)	La Jolie Ronde
Revised Guidelines and Schemes of Work for French/German/ Spanish at KS2	QCA (2007/8)	QCA
Languages for All: Languages for Life (The National Languages Strategy)	DfES (2002)	DfES
Languages: The next Generation	Nuffield Languages Inquiry (2000)	Nuffield Foundation
Languages Review	Dearing, R. and King, L. (2007)	DfES
Frames of Mind: the theory of multiple intelligences	Gardner, H. (1983)	Harvard University Press
Modern Languages in the Curriculum	Hawkins, E. (1987)	Cambridge University Press

Listening to Lorca	Hawkins, E. (1999)	CILT
Out of this nettle, dropout, we pluck this flower, opportunity	Hawkins, E. (2005) (in Language Learning Journal Vol. 32)	Association for Language Learning
Travail d'instit' – le français de la classe	Birks, R. (1994)	Didier/Hatier
The language and lore of school children	Opie, I and Opie, P. (1959)	Clarenden Press
Nürnberger Empfehlungen: Recommendations on early language learning	Goethe Institut (1996)	Goethe Institut/ Dürr and Kessler
Modern Foreign Languages in the primary school – the what, why and how of early MFL teaching	Sharpe, K. (2001)	Kogan Page
Teaching English in the Primary Classroom	Halliwell, S. (1992)	Longman
Young Learners	Phillips, S. (1992)	Oxford University Press
Ja klar!	Gerngross, G. Krenn, W. Puchta, H. (2003/4)	Eli/European Schoolbooks Ltd
Hélico	Gobbi, R. (2001)	Eli/ESB
Grandi Amici	Gerngross, G. Krenn, W. Puchta, H. (2004)	Eli/European Schoolbooks Ltd
Early Start French; Early Start Spanish; Early Start German	Rowe, I. and Kilberry, I. (2005-8)	Early Start Languages
Rigolo		Nelson Thornes
Trampoline and Le petit Trampoline	Garabédian, M., Lerasle, M. Meyer-Dreux, S. (1991/4)	Clé International
Tout le monde	Adamson, L., Buxton, G., Gardner-Medwin, N., Kent, H., McNab, R., Owen, L., Tan, S.	Heinemann

Early Language Learning DVD	CILT (2005)	CILT
European Language Portfolio – Junior Version (ELP)	CILT (2006)	CILT
A la carte	Bougard, T. and Finnie, S. (1995)	LCP
Album des monsters	Bevis, R. (1996)	LCP
Language Games Pack	Horrocks, S. (1994)	LCP
Jeux faciles, Juegos faciles, Superspiele	Cooke, C. (1991/5)	LCP
La ronde des petits: French for 3-5 year-olds	Williams, R. and Leclerq-Hallam, C. (1996)	La Jolie Ronde
Entre dans la ronde	La Jolie Ronde (1996)	La Jolie Ronde
Jeux de doigts DVD	La Jolie Ronde (2006)	La Jolie Ronde
Petit pont and Kleinbrücken	Rogers, P. (2006–2008)	Eclipse Books
Ici on parle français: French for beginners	McColl,H and Thomas, S. (1997)	MLG Publishing
Wir sprechen Deutsch: German for beginners	McColl, H. and Thomas, S. and Satchwell, P. (1999)	MLG Publishing
Se habla español : Spanish for beginners	McColl, H. and Thomas, S. and López-Ocón, T. (2000)	MLG Publishing
A world of languages	Datta, M. and Pomphrey, C. (2004)	CILT